WEIRD FOOD

WEIRD FOOD

by Joanna Emery
with illustrations by
Peter Tyler and Roger Garcia

BLUE
BIKE
BOOKS

The Publisher: Blue Bike Books
www.bluebikebooks.com

Library and Archives Canada Cataloguing in Publication

Emery, Joanna, 1966–

Weird food / Joanna Emery.

ISBN-13: 978-1-897278-38-3

   1. Food—Miscellanea. I. Title.

TX355.E47 2009   641.3   C2008-905384-2

Project Director: Nicholle Carrière
Project Editor: Nicholle Carrière
Cover Designer: Jay Dirto
Cover Image: Photos.com
Illustrations: Peter Tyler and Roger Garcia

Photography credits: Every effort has been made to accurately credit
the sources of photographs. Any errors or omissions should be
reported directly to the publisher for correction in future editions.
All photographs courtesy of Joanna Emery except the following:
© Beltsazar | Dreamstime.com (p. 41); © Moth | Dreamstime.com
(p. 110); © Piksel | Dreamstime.com (p. 84); © Prometeus |
Dreamstime.com (p. 21); © Quayside | Dreamstime.com (p. 175);
© Ryzhkov | Dreamstime.com (p. 106); © Starper | Dreamstime.com
(p. 38); © Tomonikon | Dreamstime.com (p. 117); © Valentyn75 |
Dreamstime.com (p. 195).

We acknowledge the support of the Alberta Foundation for the Arts
for our publishing program.

We acknowledge the financial support of the Government of Canada
through the Book Publishing Industry Development Program
(BPIDP) for our publishing activities.

  Canadian   Patrimoine
Heritage   canadien

PC: P1

The Weird Food Menu

ACKNOWLEDGEMENTS

A writer can always use every ounce of help available, and there are so many people I'd like to thank who helped in the creation of *Weird Food*. A heartfelt thank you to everyone at Blue Bike Books for providing me with this exciting opportunity to go with this fun and fascinating topic, to Ashley Johnson for all her speedy assistance from the office, and to my dedicated editor and publisher, Nicholle Carrière, whose expertise helped make each word on the following pages the right one.

I would also like to thank the staff at the Hamilton Public Library, in particular the Lynden Branch, for their reference assistance. As well, I'm very grateful to those who were kind enough to reply to my emails and provide some of the photographs used in this book. I hope one day I can try the delectable menus of your wonderful lands.

Last but certainly not least, a big thank you to my family, who patiently supported me throughout this project and endured my adventurous weird food sampling. Life is most definitely an exciting buffet!

dedication

To my children, Veronica, Monty and Mimi—the apples of my eye. To my husband, Greg, who cleans and cooks while I write—you're the perfect housewife. And to those I have never met but know are many around the world—the men, women and children who wonder where their next meal will come from—may those of us with enough to eat help to put food on your tables soon.

INTRODUCTION

There is no love sincerer than the love of food.

– George Bernard Shaw

If you were a wealthy Roman during the reign of Emperor Tiberius, you probably knew a fellow named Apicius. Food was Apicius' passion, and to say this affluent merchant appreciated fine dining would be an understatement. He was the first gourmand, a food-lover par excellence who even sprayed his garden lettuce with mead so it would taste like green cheesecake. Around the same time that Jesus fed the crowd of 5000 with a few loaves and fishes, Apicius threw wild parties and easily spent the equivalent of millions of dollars on extravagant banquets. When he ran out of money to pay for his food obsession, a depressed and distraught Apicius poisoned himself. Without food, he couldn't go on.

While most of us do not share Apicius' culinary addiction, none of us can live without food. To eat is a basic, universal, human need, and food is the fuel our bodies require for survival. For those of us lucky enough to afford more than a bowl of rice, food offers unlimited possibilities. Travel and trade have expanded our food knowledge. There's a brand-new world of exotic epicureanism out there, one full of fantastic food adventures, strange brews, invigorating tastes and often the most unusual dishes imaginable. This book could contain every fried or fricasseed creature ever eaten, but to do so would fill an encyclopedia set. If it fits in the mouth and can be ingested, someone has likely eaten it. Instead, these pages provide a sampling of the many weird, wacky and bizarre foods that people around the world eat. Naturally, what constitutes "weird" depends on many aspects. When the question is "What's for dinner?" the answer is likely "Whatever's available." In the Arctic, chewing on seal blubber is as normal as stir-frying a scorpion in Asia. Religious and cultural customs also dictate which foods are permissible for consumption. In Judaism and Islam, eating certain animals such as pigs or frogs is forbidden. Hindus are appalled that we eat beef (that's why cows freely roam the streets of India), but we're disgusted at the thought of consuming dog meat or drinking snake blood.

Being open to new cuisine can be a good thing. Perhaps it is similar to seeking the perfect taste, the pinnacle of gustatory delight or, in other words, a foodie nirvana. On this path to enlightenment, we encounter a range of experiences from comfort and satisfaction to excitement, passion and, occasionally, disgust. Transcendence may come, perhaps in the form of a perfectly cooked steak, a lusty risotto or maybe a Twinkie. Ultimately, it's a mysterious relationship, our love affair with food.

Which brings us back to poor Apicius. Perhaps this gastronome loved food too much for his own good, but he certainly enjoyed every delicious bite. Three centuries after his death, his name lives on in an ancient compilation of Roman recipes and the world's oldest cookbook, the *Apicius*. While some of these recipes would turn even the most adventurous celebrity chef's stomach, true food explorers relish such challenges. Whether it's tongues, stomachs, beetles or grasshoppers, they know the satisfaction that comes from trying new dishes and invite us to join the fun. "Dive in," they proclaim. "The food's great." Anyone hungry?

Recipes from the Apicius

Stuffed Sow's Belly

One full sow's belly stuffed with two crushed peppers, caraway, salt and mussels. Sew the belly tight and roast. Enjoy this with a brine sauce and mustard.

For Flamingo and Parrot

Scald the flamingo, wash and dress it, put it in a pot, add water, salt, dill, and a little vinegar. Parboil, then finish cooking with a bunch of leeks and coriander. In a mortar, crush pepper, cumin, coriander, laser root, mint and rue, moisten with vinegar, add dates and the fond of the braised bird. Thicken, strain, cover the bird with the sauce and serve. Parrot is prepared in the same manner.

CHAPTER 1

Egg-gad, Eggs!

CRACK IT OPEN

Which came first, the chicken or the egg? Perhaps it doesn't really matter, since humans eat billions of each every year. In the United States, egg production is a $300-million-a-year industry, and large-scale farms house hundreds of thousands of hens. Eggs are eaten worldwide mainly because they are an inexpensive and plentiful source of nutrition. Egg white is chock full of protein, while the yolk contains vitamins and minerals, including vitamins A and D, iron, riboflavin and thiamine. Eggs are considered an ideal food—after all, each one is meant to sustain a developing offspring. No wonder they've been a symbol of fertility and rebirth for millennia.

Think of eggs, and those oval, hard-shelled ones laid by chickens, ducks or geese come to mind. But reptiles, fish, crustaceans and even the duck-billed platypus all lay eggs. Eggs can be microscopic or bigger than a grapefruit, found in a nest of twigs or sand, or on stringy membranes clinging to a water plant. So just remember, the chicken egg is the product of a hen's ovulation, which it goes through every day or two. Without eggs, say ciao to a vital part of all-day breakfasts, soufflés and angel food cakes. Even ice cream simply isn't the same without eggs.

Whether it's a duck egg omelet, a deviled peacock egg or a raw chicken egg in a blender à la Rocky Balboa, they're delicious. Then again, eggs can be prepared in ways that make you wish you had ordered them the old-fashioned scrambled style.

Balut

Can't decide between duck or egg for a snack? Have both with *balut*, also known as the "treat with feet" or "egg with legs." Inside each shell is a fully formed duck embryo, complete with tiny beak, feet, wings, skull and eyes. Popular in Southeast Asia, you can even choose how developed you like your duck embryo (will that be 14 or 18 days worth of baby duck, sir?). Peel the shell or eat with a spoon, but watch out for those bits of crunchy bones and feathers that get caught between your teeth. Pass the dental floss, please.

1000-Year-Old Eggs

It doesn't take 1000 years to create a 1000-year-old egg, or century egg (if it did, marketing would be a nightmare), but these rubbery delicacies sure look, and smell, like they've been around for years! To make one, coat a regular duck egg with a clay-like mixture of black tea, salt, ash, charcoal and lime, then store in a cool, dark place. After several weeks, the alkaline mixture penetrates the egg, turning the white into a brownish jelly and the yolk a moldy green color. As for the smell, imagine the rottenest, most sulfurous egg stench ever and multiply that by 100. Eat these eggs sliced over tofu or chopped into a rice dish. Either way, there's no escaping one fact—these are definitely stinky old eggs!

> An egg today is better than a hen tomorrow.
> – Benjamin Franklin

Salted Eggs

Pink or red eggs stand out in the street-market stalls of China and the Philippines. The dye distinguishes them from regular fresh eggs, but inside each is a yolk that's turned a nearly neon bright orange. These salted, preserved duck and chicken eggs, or *maalat* (Filipino for "salty"), are soaked in brine, then wrapped in a damp charcoal or clay paste for a month. Make no mistake, this is one brackish snack. Tender taste buds will require mandatory rehydrating, so make sure a beverage is within arm's reach. Salted eggs are eaten with tomatoes or fish sauce, and the uncooked yolks are often used to make those delightful desserts, Chinese moon cakes.

Did You Know?

In the ninth century, eggs were banned during Lent but were highly popular at Easter celebrations.

EXTRA SMALL To EXTRA-EXTRA LARGE

Ostrich Eggs

Got a couple of hours? How about an ostrich egg for breakfast? It takes that long to hard-boil this three- to five-pound egg. Sunny-side up can be a challenge, so scrambled might be your best bet. Either way, a hammer might be required to crack this baby open. Inside is a huge, yellow-orange yolk and a virtual ocean of watery white. Each ostrich egg is the equivalent of two cartons of chicken eggs, and that sure makes a lot of meringue.

Emu Eggs

Take two boiled emu eggs, place them unshelled next to cured pork and, *voilà*, green eggs and ham! The emu egg's shell is a naturally exquisite deep green color and is often used in crafts. Like its ostrich cousin, the emu is a flightless bird that lays one hefty egg. Emus also have three toes, compared to the ostrich's two toes, and one toenail (in case you're into fried ostrich feet). Emu eggs weigh in at just over one pound each and equal 10 regular chicken eggs. The egg white cooks up spongy with a bluish (sorry, not greenish) tinge, while the abundant, thick, pale yellow yolk makes an awesome emu eggnog.

Pheasant and Quail Eggs

If ostrich and emu eggs simply don't fit in the frying pan, check out smaller alternatives. Pricey but petite, pheasant eggs are the size of a pullet's egg but with more yolk. They are low in cholesterol with a strong, but not gamey, flavor. Quail eggs are eaten worldwide, virtually anywhere these pint-sized birds can be raised, but are especially popular in the Middle East. Boil these tiny gems in tea and soy sauce for extra appeal, or crack one

into a bowl of miso soup. For teeny-weeny hors d'oeuvres, use speckled quail eggs. Peeling the shells off these hard-boiled nuggets might test anyone's patience, but they make the cutest deviled eggs on the block.

Seagull Eggs

Who would have thought the eggs of these shrieking avian dive-bombers could find their way into epicurean indulgence? Norway has always touted a good round of beer and seagull eggs as a national treat, but now these mottled, hard-boiled eggs are a sought-after delicacy in posh London restaurants and fetch about $10 each. Actually, it's not the common harbor (or urban parking lot) plopping pest variety of seagull whose eggs are in demand, but rather those of the black-headed gull. To protect the gull colonies from depletion, only licensed egg collectors can take these eggs during the few spring weeks they are in season. Authorities are also cracking down on egg thieves, who face huge fines if caught.

OTHER EGG-XAMPLES

Iguana Eggs

Rich-tasting iguana eggs are such a delicacy in Central and South America that often only the eggs are taken from the reptile. In a sort of iguana cesarean operation, live female adults are cut open to have their eggs removed. Sometimes wood ash is smeared on the wound before the iguana is released but, in many cases, the poor iguana doesn't survive. Iguana eggs are served hard-boiled or in tamales with a spicy sauce.

Turtle Eggs

Warning—it's not environmentally cool to eat turtle eggs. Sure, these ping-pong-ball-like eggs with their semi-soft shells, runny whites and grainy orange yolks have been savored for centuries. Today, however, governments worldwide from Mexico to Malaysia have laws against egg poaching (pun intended) in an effort to protect rare turtle species. In Mexico, turtle eggs are often considered an aphrodisiac and are consumed raw. To quell consumer demand for endangered turtle eggs and educate the public, posters now appear across the country featuring beautiful but scantily clad models under the bold headline: "My Man Doesn't Need To Eat Turtle Eggs."

foodie fact

To make shelling a hard-boiled egg easier, add salt to the water while the egg is cooking. How do you know know if your raw egg is fresh or old? Fresh eggs sink in water; old ones float.

EGGS OF THE SEA

Roe, Roe, Roe Your Eggs

The polite name for marine-animal eggs is roe, which certainly makes this delicacy sound more palatable. Not all roe is equal, and it varies greatly in size, color, consistency and, of course, price. Red or black lumpfish roe is relatively inexpensive, and salty cod roe can be squeezed out of a tube onto toast or crackers. Salmon roe has large, pink or orange eggs, and smelt roe is even brighter orange with a crunchy texture. Whitefish roe (known as American golden caviar) is often used as a garnish. In India, roe is deep-fried or cooked as a curry.

Herring Roe and Roe-on-Kelp

Bought fresh, canned or frozen, herring roe is ideal salted, smoked or sautéed in butter. It's not as exotic, however, as the unique herring roe-on-kelp, traditionally harvested by First Nations along the Pacific Coast. Roe-on-kelp is raw kelp seaweed coated in layers of herring roe that forms a crunchy, egg-encapsulated crust. Pan-fried, roe-on-kelp is locally known as *gow* (or *ghow*), but most of it is destined for Japan, where the salty yellow strips are traditionally served on New Year's Day. In Japanese, roe-on-kelp roughly translates into "lots of babies," which may refer either to the thousands of baby herring eggs or the legendary fertility benefits for those who eat them.

Bottarga

Move over anchovies, there's a new salty, dried fish food on the block. Known as bottarga, a word that evolved from the Arabic term for "raw fish eggs," this cured mullet roe (and sometimes that of tuna or swordfish) is popular in Mediterranean countries. The egg sacs or pouches—yes, fish ovaries—are massaged out of the fish so the membranes do not break. Then they are soaked in brine, dried and sealed in beeswax. The result is a flat, sausage-like chunk that can be sliced into thin, translucent slices or grated into various pasta dishes (for those who prefer fish reproductive organs over Parmesan cheese, anyway).

Caviar

Ah, caviar. High-society appetizer and luxury garnish. The "berries," as they are often referred to by the elite, must never be served with metal utensils as that might affect their exquisite saline taste. Remember, though,

Foodie Fact

When Italian police seized over half a million dollars worth of smuggled beluga caviar from traffickers, they were left with a dilemma—what to do with the 88 pounds of caviar before it spoiled. They decided to donate the delicacy to charitable organizations for the aged and to homeless shelters. One priest stated that the gift was welcome "even though most of the guests don't even know what those little black balls are." (Reuters, 2008).

caviar is just fish eggs—processed, unfertilized, fishy-tasting eggs. Caviar has been eaten around the world for centuries, though the best is thought to come from the Beluga sturgeon of the Caspian Sea. A small jar of these large, gray, sweetish eggs sells for around $300. Overfishing, and the fact that 90 percent of sturgeon are killed before the fish can reproduce, has put the species on the brink. Black caviar is now banned in Russia for the next decade, although Iran and Russia are still the top caviar producers.

Vegetarian? No problem. It's now possible to purchase kelp caviar, a plant-based version made from seaweed and available in three flavors. These faux fish eggs have no calories, are fat free, cholesterol free and, best of all, mucho cheaper than the real thing.

Sea Urchin Roe

Ask for an order of *uni* in Japan and out comes a plate of sushi topped with tiny golden balls. These are the edible eggs, or rather the reproductive organs, of the sea urchin, a spiny invertebrate. In Italy, sea urchins are called *ricci* or sometimes *frutta di la mare* ("fruits of the sea"), but this seaside fare is enjoyed by fishermen and epicurean connoisseurs worldwide. Split open the urchin, scrape out the orange strips and slurp them down raw or spread thickly on a baguette. With their milk-sweet taste and creamy texture, live, fresh gonads never tasted so good.

Soft Roe

Technically speaking, soft roe isn't made of fish eggs. Perhaps it shouldn't be included in this chapter, but knowledge at the fish market is everything when it comes to ordering roe. Beware! If the price sign indicates "soft roe" or "milt," what's being sold isn't from the female fish—it's from the male. That's right, this smooth, milky, white substance is none other than fish sperm in testicular sacs. Buy mouthwatering milt fresh, canned or smoked, and serve it on mini toasted crackers as hors d'oeuvres. Or try this recipe as described in the *Larousse Gastronomique*: poach the milt (soft roe) in fish stock, marinate in oil, lemon juice and cayenne pepper, then dip in batter, deep-fry and, *voilà*, soft roe fritters—a much nicer-sounding dish than fried fish balls.

Did You Know?

Since 1938, the *Larousse Gastronomique* has been the favorite gastronomy reference book for chefs and food lovers around the world.

CHAPTER 2

Bye Bye Birdy

FINGER-LICKING GOOD

Look up, way up. Is that dinner gliding across the clouds? Who cares if they're related to raptors—birds make the most heavenly dishes. They become our snacks, sandwiches and main meals. Maybe we're a little envious because they can fly, and for most of our existence, we couldn't (and still can't without the airplanes, jet packs and so on). Their fragrantly delicious meat is frequently less fatty than mammal flesh, and Americans consume around 36 billion pounds of poultry every year. Of course, all kinds of fine, feathered friends grace our tables—geese, ducks, pigeons, doves, the list goes on. In some countries, Native peoples might

eat tropical birds such as parrots and use their brilliantly colored feathers as adornment (on the other hand, many birds are smuggled for pet shops).

Throughout much of culinary history, wild birds such as quail, pheasants, partridge, swans and even wild turkeys (still a hunter's favorite today) were the best game in town. Our friendly fowl were first domesticated in India around 3200 BC. That Cajun-seasoned chicken breast you had for lunch is a chicken descendant of the red jungle fowl. Interestingly, the red jungle fowl was likely first used for cockfighting and religious rituals, not so much for meat and eggs. As for the term "fowl," it used to signify most of our large feathered friends, and "birds" were the smaller varieties. Tiny birds were eaten whole. Today, "the bird" usually means the 12-pound turkey roasting in the oven. And DNA analysis of a chicken leg has proved that Polynesians, and their chickens, set foot in the New World a century before Christopher Columbus—the first takeout drumsticks. Obviously, they preferred the thigh over the wing.

Crests

So what exactly is the red, wobbly thing on the top of a rooster's head called? If you answered a comb, coxcomb or wattle, you're on the right track, but in cooking school it's referred to as a "crest." Hens have crests, too, but they are smaller. Like virtually every other poultry part, someone once sampled a crest and declared that yes, this little bit of flesh must become a delicacy. While crests are occasionally used as garnish, *cibero* is a traditional Italian dish of chicken stew made with crests and livers.

Duck Heads and Tongues

Buckets of fried chicken are to western fast food what pails of barbecued duck heads are to Chinese street fare. The crispy skulls come already split at the top, which makes it easier to suck out the brains, eyeballs and bits of meat. In gourmet dishes, the head and feet are still attached to the rest of the bird, and the duck head is often reserved for the guest of honor. If this happens to be you, try the tongue first, as it's the choicest piece. These chewy chunks with a strip of cartilage down the middle are also served separately in black bean sauce or barbecued like a mummified tongue on a stick. Enjoy, and try not to think about the poor, quackless ducks.

Giblets and Gizzards

Have you ever bought a fresh turkey only to find a plastic bag of "parts" stuffed in its cavity? These are the giblets (bird offal) and usually consist of the bird's heart, liver, neck bone and gizzard. Grandmas around the world fry up giblets for home-cooked casseroles and stuffing, but maybe they never explained what these tender tidbits used to be. So what exactly is a gizzard? Because birds don't have teeth, they often ingest tiny pebbles to grind up their food in a muscular little pouch called the gizzard. In other words, eating a gizzard is like stomaching a stomach.

Did You Know?

Chicken feathers aren't just for duvets and pillows. New technology is now being used to process the feathers and quills into biodegradable plastic products. The protein found in quills can also be made more digestible for use in animal feed or even dietary supplements for humans — good news for bodybuilders with scrawny chicken legs.

Bird's Nest Soup

Soup's on, and it's full of spit. Believe it or not, nests made with bird saliva have been part of Asian cuisine for over 400 years. Depending on the quality of the nest, the exotic soup made from these nests can cost up to $300 a bowl. It takes the male cave swift (or "swiflet") over a month to stick bits of twigs and leaves together with his spittle into a small, peach-sized nest. Regulated nest-gatherers perform the perilous job of collecting these nests from the seaside rock walls in countries such as Indonesia, Thailand and the Philippines. While governments enforce licensing in order to protect the swifts, poachers and unscrupulous harvesters lured by big bucks often don't care if eggs or chicks are present in the nests. China imports most of the world's edible birds' nests for sale in herbal stores and restaurants. The dried, translucent nests must be soaked either in sugar water, if they are to be made into a dessert, or a salty broth with ginger and onion. Edible birds' nests reputedly boost the immune system and are traditionally served to the sick and elderly. If the thought of eating bird spittle fails to activate your salivary glands, you can always buy mock bird's nest soup, which is made of fish maw and seaweed strands.

Owl Soup

Does eating owl keep you up all night? Does anyone give a hoot? Although many owls are now protected species, Native cultures and our forefathers would undoubtedly have eaten them. In 19th-century Britain, homemade owl soup was thought to cure whooping cough. Today, owl isn't exactly a popular poultry in North America, but it is still eaten in other cultures. There is the unfortunate story of a British ornithologist, who in 1996 went in search of the rare rufous fishing owl. With a mere 30 sightings on record, this small bird only appears in a specific region of Africa, so the consummate expert traveled to a remote Nigerian village, where he asked the locals about the elusive fishing owl. After viewing photographs, the locals said yes, they had seen the owl. In fact, they had eaten it for breakfast.

CHIRPY DELIGHTS

Songbirds

If reincarnation does exist, do not, repeat, do not come back as an ortolan. Some 30,000 of these cute, chirpy songbirds were once poached every year in France for a traditional dish. The logistics behind an ortolan entrée are not so appetizing. Once the bird is captured, it is left in a dark box for days with nothing but an endless supply of millet, grapes and insects. All the bird can do is gorge itself until it literally quadruples in size and resembles those laughable obese animals on useless Internet sites. The fattened bird is then drowned in Armagnac brandy and roasted, but the worst (and strangest) is yet to come. The diner bites off the ortolan's head and beak and eats the body whole. All of this is done while the diner's head is covered with a cloth napkin. The napkin, by tradition, assists the diner as he or she inhales the ambrosial ortolan aromas, though other theories regarding this odd practice are that a) perhaps the diner doesn't want to be identified, or b) the diner is praying for forgiveness from the little bird. To protect the species, ortolan hunting was banned in 1999, but that didn't stop former French president François Mitterand from supposedly feasting on ortolan days before he died of cancer. Which logically poses the question, is it divine karma if he is now chirping his head off as a reincarnated ortolan?

Muttonbird

If only roast leg of lamb could fly. Some believe it does, as the muttonbird. Despite its name, this native Australian seabird, which also goes by the name of short-tailed shearwater, doesn't taste like mutton. It tends towards a fishier flavor more reflective of its seafood diet. Generations ago, a larger muttonbird relative was dubbed the "flying sheep" by early settlers. When that unlucky bird was gobbled into extinction, the shearwater was hailed as the new muttonbird. Today, the harvest of muttonbird chicks for their feathers, flesh and oil is strictly controlled, but you can still find muttonbird meat in local specialty stores, right next to the spring lamb.

Ostrich and Emu

An ostrich drumstick? Now there's a conversation starter at any family picnic. The towering flightless ostrich and its smaller cousin, the emu, have long been traditional foods in their native Africa and Australia, respectively. Both are now farmed extensively in North America for their meat, eggs, leather and, in the case of the emu, for its oil. Ostrich meat has a deep red color, is low in fat, high in calcium and actually tastes more like lean beef than poultry. Ditto for emu (some might call it "ostrich lite"), though emu has a gamier flavor and is best eaten on the rare side.

Did You Know?

Fancy a turducken this Thanksgiving? You'll need extra cranberry sauce. It's a chicken stuffed into a duck stuffed into a turkey (all carefully deboned) — in other words, layered poultry.

Peacock

Originally from the Middle East, this fashionable pheasant was the decorative centerpiece of medieval banquets and festivals for centuries. Great care was taken to preserve the peacock's exotic plumage during preparation. The bird was skinned of its feathers and roasted with the head covered in a wet cloth to protect the delicate crest. Once cooked, the peacock was shoved back into its skin, arranged on a platter and paraded out for the feast. Nowadays, finding peacock at a local supermarket is a huge challenge. They're usually only kept as decorative poultry, but if you do come across one, you'll know exactly how to impress your dinner guests.

Pigeon

You might think of these bobbing birdies as city pests, but they've been a large part of diets around the world for centuries. Street vendors in various Asian cities sell skewered baby pigeons as a sort of "pigeon kebab," and in the West, assorted pigeon dishes usually call for the younger birds, also known as squabs. Stuffed with chopped liver, herbs and seasoning, squabs can be baked into a hearty pigeon pie. While not a current popular poultry, domesticated pigeons and doves are still raised by hobbyists, and occasionally for their meat. For those who complain about pigeon droppings on downtown streets, a pigeon recipe revival might be the answer. In the past, pigeon hunting was once a regular activity. So widespread, in fact, that one type of pigeon suffered a tragic outcome. Remember the passenger pigeon? This once-common bird had the unfortunate characteristics of being both easy to catch and delicious. Like the dodo, humans literally ate it to extinction!

> The toes of the pigeon for roasting should be cut off.
> – Eliza Acton, English poet and cook, 1845

Roast Pigeon Brains

Recent studies indicate that pigeons may actually be slightly more intelligent than the average three-year-old. The bird's brains, however, are definitely not as big. It takes more than a few avian cerebellums to make roast pigeon brains, a dish consumed in China and other parts of the world. First, the bird brains are soaked in water to let the blood seep out, then roasted with a few spices. Pigeon brains have not yet caught on in North America, but wrap these unique morsels in bacon, and they could be a groovy appetizer and conversation starter: "Hello, may I pick your brains?"

Puffin

With its down-turned beak and tuxedo-style coloring, it's hard to imagine why anyone would want to eat a lovable little puffin. In Iceland, however, they catch these squat birds like butterflies in large, handheld nets (called sky fishing for seabirds). For those who aren't into swinging at puffins, they can be ordered on gourmet menus in the country. Still, it is hard to ignore the thought of those puffins clinging to their cliffs trying not to get caught. In that case, try a less endearing relative of the puffin, a large auk called the guillemot.

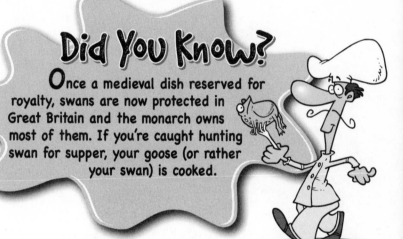

Did You Know?

Once a medieval dish reserved for royalty, swans are now protected in Great Britain and the monarch owns most of them. If you're caught hunting swan for supper, your goose (or rather your swan) is cooked.

CHAPTER 3

Tastes Like Chicken

SLITHERY THROAT-SLIDERS

Scaly or smooth, often scary and always cold-blooded until they're cooked, most reptiles and amphibians remind us of their dinosaur ancestors far more than feathery birds ever could. It's understandable that we don't automatically smack our lips whenever we see one. Stamping out a Godzilla look-a-like is one thing, gulping the creature down is quite another. Surprisingly, most are edible, and their flesh quite palatable, while others fall into the ubiquitous "poultry-like" category if we'd only give them a try. Take snake, for instance. It's hard not to wince at the way these reptiles are prepared in Asia, often dispatched right before your eyes, but grilled rattlesnake, lizards and alligator can be found in many parts of America as well. Frogs aren't merely survival food, either. They're gourmet morsels at the fanciest restaurants and, along with other amphibians, have become adventurous eating for those looking to fancy up an everyday meal.

Snake

Think of slinky snake as the "other white meat." It is the yang, the masculine and the positive in Chinese yin and yang. Various Asian restaurants keep live snakes on hand, ready to be killed for a sweet, mild-tasting reptilian entrée (freshness is an important aspect of Chinese cuisine). First, the head is cut off. If the snake is a venomous species, this is done very carefully. Then the snake is stripped of its skin, which is saved to be later dried, powdered and used in herbal remedies. Next, the skinless snake is rinsed and filleted of the little rib bones that attach to the spine. The meat can be slivered or chopped into finger-sized pieces ready to be battered, deep-fried or sautéed in wine or as a hotpot. This method involves a pot of boiling water placed in the center of a table and surrounded by an arrangement of meat, ginger, spices, vegetables and noodles. Guests dip the raw meat into the water until done in a type of "cook-it-yourself" service.

Rattlesnake

Barbecued rattlesnake conjures up images of cowboys sitting by an open fire under a starry desert sky. Rather romantic for a meat that's described as bony with a fishy taste, somewhere between alligator fillet and frog legs. The good news is that snake is all muscle—no fat or tendons to worry about, just bones. Popular in the southwest U.S. and Mexico, rattlesnake fetches almost $60 a pound in Europe at the fanciest restaurants. Rattlesnake can be used in many recipes as a substitute for pork, chicken or seafood. Boil the filleted snake for an hour first to remove the bones, especially if it's going to be used in a chili. Alternately, cut the snake in three- or four-inch lengths and grill, then spit out the bones as you eat.

Did You Know?

The female rattlesnake gives birth to live young, and these snakes can live about 20 years.

> Always carry a large flagon of whisky in case of snakebite and, furthermore, always carry a small snake.
>
> – W.C. Fields

Iguana

Grilled or skewered, these green leapin' lizards are called "chicken of the trees" in Central America and Mexico. They can be roasted, baked with a chili sauce in tamales or served in stews. What do they taste like? Some say turkey (as opposed to chicken). Iguanas can grow up to six feet in length, including the long tail. Even though iguanas are protected in many areas, they are still eaten, especially during Easter in Nicaragua, where they make a specialty soup with rice or *pinol*, an edible paste thought to cure common illnesses.

> What is food to one man may be be fierce poison to others.
>
> – Lucretius, 1st century BC

Chuckwalla

The trick to a gourmet chuckwalla dinner is to first successfully catch this foot-and-a-half-long vegetarian desert lizard. It hides from predators by crawling into the crevices between rocks, then gulping air to expand its potbelly to become wedged there. Found in Mexico and the southern U.S., the chuckwalla is best prepared the way it has been cooked for centuries—roasted in its skin, on a stick, over an open fire.

Salamander

Salamanders have been eaten for centuries, but some species are on the slippery slope to disappearance. Take the foot-long axolotl, for example. Caught and cooked since Aztec days, this Mexican amphibian is now threatened with extinction. On the other side of the world, the nocturnal Chinese giant salamander faces a similar peril. As the world's largest amphibian, it is over five feet in length, has a massive, broad head with beady eyes, wrinkly mucus-covered skin and could pass as the Loch Ness monster's long-lost relative. Would anyone want to eat Nessie's little brother? The answer, unfortunately, is yes, mainly because this hefty salamander is an illegal delicacy in Asia and fetches almost $60 a pound. Overhunting, along with pollution and loss of habitat, has put the giant salamander on the endangered list since 1976. Although it can live up to 50 years, most giant salamanders on the black market are much younger and not nearly as humongous as their name suggests.

Alligator

You've heard of alligator shoes and purses, but have you tried alligator steaks? There are also alligator burgers, wings (actually part of the leg), sausage, pepperettes and even jerky. Native to the U.S. and China, these creatures can grow up to 19 feet long, including the tail. Alligator meat has been described as a cross between fish and chicken, and it is low in calories. The pinker body meat is medium-tough, like cheaper cuts of pork, while the tail consists of veal-like white meat. No matter how it's prepared, alligator is one toothsome meat.

Did You Know?

Jerky, a dried, seasoned meat, was first eaten in England in 1612 by John Smith, who described it as "jerkin beef."

Crocodile

Eat or be eaten? When faced with a crocodile, that may be the choice. Every once in a while, the news media in Australia report that a crocodile has eaten someone. This reptile's meat, however, is white, succulent, low in fat and high in protein. If this sounds like the perfect bite, it just may be. Welcome to crocodile cuisine. Most crocodile is imported from Australia, New Zealand or African countries, and many are farmed, but crocodile aficionados say the meat is worth it. Crocodile pie is considered "bush tucker" in Australia and tastes like gristly chicken. Other chow-down dishes include crocodile soup, crocodile palm (another name for the foot), fried crocodile and crocodile curry. Choose young crocodile tail and legs for the most tender parts.

Crocodile Schnitzels

9 ounces crocodile fillets, sliced thinly
1/2 cup minced walnuts
1 cup breadcrumbs
1 cup flour
1 cup milk
1 egg

Dust fillets with flour. Dip in egg wash (1 egg beaten with 1 cup milk). Blend walnuts and breadcrumbs and coat crocodile with crumb mixture. Fry in preheated mixture of oil and butter. Serve with Tropical Fruit Sauce (below).

(Reprinted with permission from WildRecipes.com.)

Tropical Fruit Sauce

1 large mango, diced
1 pawpaw, diced
3 Tbsp brown sugar
3 Tbsp butter
3 Tbsp chopped walnuts
1 Tbsp rum, brandy or whiskey (optional)
1 cup water

Melt butter in pan and sauté walnuts. Add sugar and stir for two minutes. Add mango and pawpaw and mash. Add water and stir occasionally until mixture boils. Stir in spirits, reduce heat and simmer for 15 minutes.

(Reprinted with permission from WildRecipes.com.)

Gecko

These small lizards hardly seem worth the trouble. They vary from only a few inches to almost half a foot long, but it would take several to make a decent meal. The tinier ones are deep-fried whole, and bigger ones can be filleted and grilled. In Vietnam and other parts of Asia, geckos also make an appearance in bottles of alcohol or in powdered form, to be taken as a traditional medicine. A lucky few are kept alive and sold as pets.

Snails

A friend once mentioned that he was clearing out his garden and found tons of snails hidden behind a wall. What began as a dare to gross out the kids turned into a recipe for snails in garlic and parsley butter. Snails have been eaten since Roman times, and today, two out of every three snails consumed worldwide are eaten in France, and not only by curious tourists. They are, of course, known in French as *escargots*. The cream of the snail crop is the large and meaty Burgundy snail, which makes

the best escargots. Snails used for this famous French dish are a protected species in France. Since there is a shortage of wild snails, most are imported from Eastern Europe. Non-cultivated snails don't even get a sympathetic last meal. They must be starved for a week so their digestive systems aren't full of any unsavory gunk. Once boiled, they're removed from their shells and turned into grilled snails or snails in white wine sauce. Naturally, it's easier to buy snails in a can. Either way, escargots are not meant to be scoffed down, but rather teased out of their shells and rolled in the mouth, at a snail's pace.

Did You Know?

Heliculture is the practice of raising snails for food.

Snail Liver Pâté

What do you do with snail livers? Can you even locate a snail's liver? It's located in the snail's mantle, which contains other organs and is the tastiest part of this slow-mover. The livers of Burgundy snails are inedible, but one Czech company turns the minute organ of the larger North African variety into a unique, and pricey, snail liver pâté. Steeped in sunflower oil, this pâté is the company's bestseller, although they also sell snail caviar—tiny, white snail eggs mixed with pickle juice.

Winkle

A 19th-century cookery book calls these nutty, sweet mini-snails "food among the poorer classes." The popularity of winkles as a Lilliputian pleasure has greatly declined in England and Europe, but families can still be seen "winkle picking" while on seaside holidays. Whether eaten cold and raw, or boiled in salted water, winkles need to be carefully picked out of their whorled shells with a pin. Spread onto buttered bread, they're a welcome change from the old sardine standby.

DO THE FROG KICK

Frog Legs

Fried, breaded or steamed with butter and herbs, frog legs are as much a part of French culinary culture as baguettes, but they are also trendy in Chinese restaurants. Frog legs have even been unearthed in archaeological sites dating back to 2900 BC. Each frog leg looks, and tastes, somewhat like a chicken wing but is actually the upper joint of the hind leg, which contains one bone and strands of meat. For cuisine, the legs are served together as a pair. France imports approximately 4000 tons of frog legs every year. Most come from Indonesia—numbered in the millions. Animal rights activists have fought back with various "Have Pity on the Frogs" campaigns, but so far demand for the classic cuisine remains high, and there have been no sightings of little amphibians in pint-sized wheelchairs. Bangladesh once exported huge numbers of frog legs until they noticed a huge increase in the fly population. Not surprisingly, they put nature's flycatcher on the "no buy" list.

Hasma

Also called frog cream, frog fat or frog roe, *hasma* is a relatively uncommon but traditional Asian treat. The tapioca-like blobs, or "snow jelly," that float around in this sweet dessert are actually the ovary fat and fallopian tubes of the grass, or "winter," frog (it is often caught just before wintertime). Herbal vendors sell this white, grainy membrane either frozen or dried, but hasma costs a pretty penny. Once the dish of emperors and royalty, it is thought to be good for the complexion, coughs and the occasional frog in the throat.

Did You Know?

Love 'em or hate 'em, frogs have turned up on many a banquet plate throughout the centuries. Ancient Chinese dynasties served boiled frogs still clinging to their bamboo shoots. Today, whole frogs are deep-fried, skewered, grilled and spiced up nicely—nothing is wasted. Toads, on the other and, are rather warty and have shorter legs. They're not a high-demand food, at least not in Europe. When even your dog spits out a frothy toad, you know these amphibians aren't exactly prime rib.

Frog Sashimi

Sashimi is a Japanese style of serving raw fish, so an order of frog sashimi is, that's right, raw frog meat. Don't be surprised if you're served a recently living frog (the still-beating heart gives that away).

Giant Ditch Frog

This chunky amphibian used to leap happily around most Caribbean islands but is now limited to Dominica and Montserrat. The reason, evidently, is because island inhabitants couldn't resist frying up the giant ditch frog every time it hopped by. More than a few croaked and were turned into a dish, the name of which, "mountain chicken," describes its appealing flavor.

SLOW COOKIN'

Turtle Soup

Got a pond? Why not try turtle for dinner? Then again, catching one of these slimy, algae-covered amphibians can be a turnoff. Shelling the poor thing is another matter, but the white back meat discovered underneath is heavenly when grilled. Although some endangered turtles, such as the sea turtle, make certain dishes illegal, turtle or snapper soup is still on American menus. The meat can be bought frozen, then chopped up and cooked with beans, corn and tomatoes to make a thick, brownish broth. The turtle soup served in more eastern countries is usually clear. Mock turtle soup uses beef, veal or organ meats instead of turtle. This faux soup originated in the mid-18th century, when they used meat from a calf's head to simulate the turtle chunks. To check whether or not your real turtle soup is authentic, look for a greenish or yellow fatty substance floating in the broth. It is the part where the meat attaches to the shell.

Did You Know?

In 1840, turtle soup was served as an appetizer at Queen Victoria's Christmas dinner.

Turtle Jelly

Scour the shelves of Chinatown markets, and you'll likely find a box or can of turtle jelly (it's the one with the picture of the turtle on the package). No worries—this brownish-black *guilinggao* jelly, as it is called, usually doesn't actually contain any turtle. Sold as a dessert and often for its health and medicinal properties, it also makes a great Halloween treat, especially in bat-shaped jelly molds.

CHAPTER 4

Meet the Meat

WILD THINGS

Meat makes the meal, or at least that's what many non-vegetarians think at dinnertime. Humans have been devouring cooked flesh ever since our caveman ancestors accidentally dropped some raw mammoth slabs into a fire pit. Grill-marked steaks, properly "barred and charred," may be a badge of manliness, but more often than not, it's the hearty meat 'n' potato stews of our childhoods that bring us the most comfort. In times of war or famine, however, almost any meat will do. If it's tender and nutritious, does it matter where it came from? Compared to most plants, meat is a good source of protein, and all-you-can-eat-buffet experts (except the vegan ones) would be quite bored without an endless variety of meaty menu options. The top four meats consumed around the world are beef, pig, sheep and goat. That said, the average American frequently asks "Where's the beef?" He or she obviously finds it, since each of us eats about 200 pounds of red meat every year—far more than what our bodies require or is necessarily healthy. Most people are surprised to learn that a single hamburger from a fast-food restaurant may contain meat from hundreds of different cows—something to chew on when your next burger attack hits.

> Red meat is not bad for you. Now blue-green meat, that's bad for you!
>
> – Tommy Smothers

Bush Meat vs. Bush Tucker

When you're hungry, a bird in the hand really is worth two in the bush. Bush meat includes wild game such as birds, reptiles and mammals in remote, untamed areas of countries in Africa or South America. Apes, monkeys, anything—if it can be caught and cooked, it's meat. In Australia, "tucker" means food, and "bush tucker" usually refers to native grub that has been eaten for thousands of years, including wild fruit, greens, nuts or insects and animals such as kangaroo. There's no beating around the bush—these foods aren't your typical grocery store provisions, but when it comes to sustenance, they'll fill your belly.

Gorilla and Monkeys

For most of us, the thought of eating an ape or monkey is almost the equivalent of devouring a second cousin. Any cooked body parts that eerily resemble hairy versions of our own are way too close for comfort. Poachers, however, don't care if these primates share most of our DNA. Unlike tribes of the past who hunted with spears or arrows, today's poachers kill indiscriminately with modern rifles. The result is a sharp decline in the ape population, with more gorillas and monkeys hunted each year for food than are held in zoos around the world. Most of these primates, such as the silverback gorilla, are protected species, but that doesn't stop the slaughter. This exotic bush meat fetches a high price in village markets across Congo, Cameroon, Gabon and other African countries. Even gorilla hands and feet are considered delicacies. Ironically, the same markets often sell orphaned baby monkeys as pets, the mother having been shot for meat. Fortunately, there are wildlife organizations that try to rehabilitate orphaned animals, but it is a challenge in countries where any kind of meat is almost a luxury item.

Elephant

How do you eat an elephant? One bite at a time.

It's an old joke, but a single elephant really can feed a small village for months. The pygmies of Congo used poisoned spears to bring down the world's largest land mammal, and when food was scarce during the Siege of Paris (Franco-Prussian War) in 1870, elephants suspiciously disappeared from zoos and no doubt ended up on dinner plates. Although protected, elephants are still eaten occasionally in parts of Africa and Thailand. Poachers cut off the valuable ivory tusks but also char the meat to preserve it on its way to the black market. In countries where the average income is barely a dollar a day, the meat of one endangered forest elephant can fetch upwards of $6000. Lean and low in fat, elephant meat has been likened to moose or buffalo with gamey overtones. It is supposedly chewy, like a huge slice of beef tongue, with the trunk and feet being the tastiest parts—if you enjoy gnawing on wrinkly leather trunks found in dusty attics, that is.

Classic Elephant Stew Recipe (Author Unknown)

1 medium-sized elephant
2 hares
Gravy

Chop elephant into bite-size pieces (this could take some time) and cover with gravy.
Cook over a fire pit for about three weeks at 450°F.
This recipe serves approximately 3500 guests.
If more guests are expected, add the two hares.
Do this only if necessary, as most people do not like to find a hare in their stew.

A Mammoth Discovery

Ten thousand years ago, early Americans dined on mammoth and mastodon meat. Now we have an idea of where they put the leftovers. When his friend's horse died, one paleontologist knew he had the perfect opportunity to test his theory that ancient peoples used frozen lakes to store meat. He broke the ice on a nearby pond and threw in hunks of weighted-down horsemeat. For months, he was able to fish out some meat, then cook and eat it without any ill effects. As the weather became warmer, bacteria similar to that found in cheese and yogurt grew in the meat and protected it from deadly microbes. The meat remained perfectly safe to eat, even if it did end up the equivalent of smelly, wet cheese. (*Scientific American*, April 2000).

Kangaroo

Down Under bouncy burgers and kanga-banga sausages are among the many different ways to serve up kangaroo. This marsupial's low-fat meat has been described as being similar to venison and can be easily smoked, seared or thrown on the barbie. Indigenous Australians and early settlers ate it as a staple, but today the hunting and farming of kangaroos is controlled, although this unusual livestock actually provides an environmentally friendly meat. Their hopping hindquarters don't damage the land like cattle and sheep hooves, and their digestive systems don't produce the ubiquitous methane gas emissions (yes, we're talking about the farts and burps of most domesticated herds). Kangaroo meat has even been given a new name—australus—in an effort to make it more palatable to the general public. As of now, widespread farming of kangaroo has not yet made it big, perhaps because most people don't want to barbecue Skippy, and the thought of those little baby joeys carried around in their mother's pouches is simply way too cute to digest.

Wallaby

Think a kangaroo is too adorable to eat? Check out a wallaby. This nocturnal creature looks like a toddler kangaroo and, while not readily available, legal wallaby meat does appear on some Australian menus as well as in markets in Germany and France. Known as the "veal of kangaroo," wallaby meat is a burgundy color, with a delicate, fine texture. Dishes include wallaby steaks, wallaby pie, wallaby kebabs and even wallaby salami. It's enough to make one wallow over the fate of such cuddly creatures.

Camel

To roast a camel, you need one humongous spit. And don't pick a stressed out male bull seeking a mate, as its meat turns dark purple and has an unappetizing flavor. Camel cooking tips have been around for over 1500 years. That's how long these desert beasts of burden have been ending up on dinner plates, albeit as a delicacy, since it doesn't make much sense to eat an important mode of transportation. Camels also provide nutritious milk, which is high in vitamin C and perfect for camel yogurt. The humps store fat for energy, not water as is often thought. There's flavor in those fatty tissues, and the humps can be eaten raw but are usually boiled or cut into cubes and deep-fried. You can even buy battered camel hump in select Beijing restaurants, for a price, of course. Camel ribs and loins resemble tough beef but can be made into camel burgers or camel jerky with enough chew in it to last for a long ride off into the sunset.

Did You Know?

Camel was listed on a Christmas Eve menu in Paris in 1870.

Bear

Its pelt makes a beautiful rug in front of the fireplace, but what happens to the rest of the bear? Hunters often eat this sweetish meat, and Native peoples have included it in their diet for thousands of years. Like pork, bear meat should be well cooked as it can contain *Trichinella*, a roundworm that causes illness. In China, bear is much rarer but is prized for its gallbladder and bile, which is thought to enhance virility. Bear paw meat is another odd delicacy; it is boiled in water for hours until the meat falls off the bone, then it is sliced and served. Beware of polar bear liver, though, as it contains so much vitamin A that it is toxic. Although dwindling polar bear numbers are worrisome, that hasn't stopped foreign sportsmen from hiring Native guides and paying thousands of dollars to hunt polar bears. The practice is strictly regulated, but dozens are still killed every year.

Reindeer

Rudolph pizza, anyone? Reindeer meat can be found on menus in Alaska, Norway, Sweden, Russia and parts of Canada. Known as caribou in North America, these deer of the far north are hunted by the Inuit for their hides, antlers and meat. Today, hunting is used to control their populations, but reindeer are also farmed. Care to sample reindeer pot roast, reindeer milk or reindeer sausage? In Scandinavian countries, you can even buy sautéed reindeer, canned reindeer and reindeer pâté. Reindeer is identical to lean venison, with three times more protein than beef, but it's hard for North American culture to get around the idea of eating the lead guide of Santa's sleigh. A case in point is the Swedish astronaut who was not allowed to bring dried reindeer on board the space shuttle during a mission scheduled close to Christmas. After a little delicate diplomacy, he brought moose instead.

Muskox

Described as rather gamey and greasier than regular beef, the meat of a muskox is definitely unique. Come to think of it, doesn't a muskox look like a sheep on steroids? Perhaps it comes as no surprise, then, that many people liken muskox meat to mutton. Thanks to locally hunted fare, muskox stew or muskox burgers still make the menus of some northern communities.

Yakking About Yaks

Domesticated for over 3000 years, these horned bovines are the milk and meat machines of mountainous Asian regions. Yaks, nicknamed "grunting oxen," provide a deep red meat with little marbling and one-sixth the fat of beef. Tibetans eat the juicy yak meat boiled, dried, powdered and even raw. Shaggy beasts of burden, yaks are famous for their treks across the Himalayas, although wild yaks are in danger of becoming extinct.

Did You Know?

A Pennsylvania man took over four and half hours to finish what was quite possibly the world's largest hamburger. Served at a pub in Pennsylvania, this super-sized burger began as 15 pounds of (lean) ground beef and five pounds of toppings, including lettuce, cheese, tomatoes, onions and banana peppers, along with one cup each of ketchup, mustard, relish and mayonnaise (in total, about 18,790 calories). He likely did not order fries with his burger. (Associated Press, 2008).

Bison

You say buffalo, I say bison. Before Europeans arrived, between 30 and 60 million bison, also known as American buffalo, were at home on the range and roamed freely across North America. Unfortunately, by 1890, overhunting had reduced their numbers to less than 1000. Today, these bovines have been brought back from near extinction and are quickly becoming an attractive alternative to beef. Bison farms tout their free-range product as a lean meat high in omega-3 essential fatty acids. Try the rich, sweet meat western-style as buffalo ribs or the more gourmet bison carpaccio cold cut.

Recipe for Pemmican

You, too, can feel like a wilderness fur trader with this tasty, high-energy food. Here's how to make your own pemmican:

> Grind or pulverize several pounds of dried buffalo meat until it is almost powder. If you can't find buffalo meat, deer, caribou or beef will do. Add a few cups of dried, ground fruit or berries (rosehips or saskatoons are traditional). Melt a couple of cups of rendered buffalo (or beef) fat and combine with the meat and berry mixture. Add unsalted nuts or honey for extra flavor. Bag the mixture in Ziplocs (if you have animal-hide bags, even better). Enjoy this year, next year and the next...

Nutria

Nutria, nutrition—is it a mere coincidence that these two words sound so similar? Also called coypu, nutria are not native to the U.S., but a few were once brought over from South America and, like happy, vacationing rodents do, they multiplied. Now, some states such as Louisiana are actively promoting nutria hunts to help preserve the wetlands that these large, swimming rodents tend to damage. The meat is similar to rabbit, with the taste of dark turkey meat, and it can be used in various recipes such as nutria chili, stuffed nutria hindquarters and nutria sausage.

Bat

Bat legs resemble skinny chicken wings, and the meat is dark with a beef-like taste, but many think of bat as a mouth-watering morsel, if you don't mind eating a flying, mosquito-killing rodent. Even rocker Ozzy Osborne said bat was "crunchy and warm," albeit he thought he was biting the head off a fake one. Bat soup is a delicacy in Cambodia, as is roast fruit bat, but throughout Southeast

Asia, you can find the occasional bat blood drink, drained fresh in front of your eyes. Bat bodies don't contain a lot of meat, so the barbecued kind (either skinned or with the hair singed off) is meant to be eaten whole—wings, teeth and all. Even cooked, the males have a more distinctive smell and flavor than the females. The Chamorros people of Guam often ate these little mammals boiled in coconut cream. Unknown to them, the bats had previously dined on a certain plant seed that contained a neurotoxin linked to a brain disease. After numerous cases of the disease, a link was made, and bats ceased to be a large part of the tribe's diet.

Did You Know?

The Pemba flying fox, a fruit bat with a five-foot wingspan, was so widely hunted and eaten on its native island near Tanzania that by the 1990s, only a few specimens remained. Thanks to conservation efforts, the bat is now off the menu and the critically endangered list, and local people attend "Pemba flying fox clubs" instead of bat buffets.
(msnbc.com)

ROADKILL, THE ULTIMATE MYSTERY MEAT

It is illegal to give someone food in which has been found a dead mouse or weasel.

– Ancient Irish Law

Armadillos

They're called "Texas speed bumps" for a reason. These rabbit-sized creatures are known for their ill-fated attempts to cross highways as they hobble around the southern U.S., Mexico and Central and South America. An armadillo has a tendency to stand its ground on the road until the last minute, when it jumps up to four feet in the air, right into a vehicle's grill. The other kind of "grilled armadillo" makes a much better dish, as does armadillo chili. Catching one, though, is no easy feat, since the animal curls up into a ball when afraid and is protected by its tough outer armor. Armadillo meat is said to be a good substitute for pork but needs to be cooked thoroughly to destroy any parasites. During the Depression era, the critters were associated with poorer folk, and armadillos were often referred to as "Hoover hogs" after President Herbert Hoover.

Did You Know?

Armadillos give birth to identical quadruplets yearly.

Opossum

These nocturnal mammals probably won't end up as the
next drive-thru (or rather drive-over) sensation. Their
flesh isn't exactly ideal for fast food, although the odds
of hitting one on the highway are high. Many acciden-
tal opossum killers wonder if the meat is worth taking
home for dinner. If you don't mind eating something that
looks like pale gray housecat, it could be. Like raccoons,
beavers, skunks, porcupines and groundhogs, opossums
have a greasy taste and should be cooked slowly, or at
least parboiled before roasting. Once done, place the critter on a dish surrounded by potatoes and present it as
country-baked opossum. For a little comic relief, why not
attach a tiny sign that says, "I'm not dead, just playing
possum"? Then again, maybe that wouldn't go down too
well with your dinner guests.

Skunk

Skunk potpie must smell better than it sounds or this
settlers' dish would not have survived to the present day.
According to handed-down recipes, the preferred method
of skunk hunting is to drown the potentially odiferous
animal first, no doubt to prevent it from stinking to high
heaven. Before cooking, remove the scent sack below the
tail to keep Pepé le Pew as palatable as possible. Save
the soft black-and-white hide for a pair of trendy furry
gloves, and enjoy the rest as roasted hillbilly fare.

Porcupine

One of the most important steps to remember when preparing roast porcupine is to pluck those prickly quills—they don't go down well if accidentally ingested. Also remove the rear scent glands, as well as the head and those front paws with their tiny, human-like hands. Porcupine is eaten rurally in parts of Africa and North America, and was a traditional food for North American Native peoples, who used the quills to decorate ceremonial objects and clothing. Similar to duck, the sweetish, flavorful meat can be made into a curry, barbecued or stuffed and baked like a roast. Oh, and those porcupine meatballs frequently mentioned in cookbooks across the country? Sorry, but they're just regular beef or pork mixed with rice and made into balls—no porcupine meat included.

Raccoon

Would you like fries with your roadkill? An upscale Chicago restaurant features a raccoon dish that looks like it was run over, including a yellow stripe down the middle of the plate. Coon connoisseurs swear by the sweet, succulent meat and recommend that it be marinated before it is cooked on a barbecue or in a stew. Skinned raccoons fetch about five dollars per carcass according to the Illinois Department of Natural Resources. The masked varmints are especially in demand prior to Thanksgiving and other holidays, as well as on Super Bowl Sunday.

Groundhog

If the scent of roasted varmint wafts through the log cabin, it may be Groundhog Day. Groundhogs, also known as woodchucks, were once a common rural food in the 19th century. They're currently relegated to the status of bucktoothed pest since they eat whatever vegetation they can find, including your lawn, and dig tunnels anywhere there's soil, including golf courses. Groundhogs hibernate during the winter and frequently end up as roadkill or pellet-gun target practice the rest of the year. They're edible, although the flesh tends to be greasy, mainly because groundhogs are a type of marmot. Think overgrown squirrel, minus the bushy tail and acorn fetish.

Squirrel

The next time one of these suicidal rodents with the bushy tail darts in front of your car, think of a heaping plate of squirrel brains scrambled with eggs for dinner. Or how about a hearty pot of Brunswick stew? It's a tomato-based southern dish chock full of lima beans, corn, vegetables and, well, squirrel meat. Sure, the squirrels are finicky to skin and there isn't much meat on their tiny bones, but what you can pick off tastes just like the meat of a nut-fed rabbit. Here's a hint—go for the younger squirrels, as their meat isn't as tough and doesn't leave an electrical-wire aftertaste in your mouth. Enjoy every bite of your freebie meal. In the UK, fancy restaurants catering to radical diners now offer squirrel and mushroom pie or braised squirrel with walnuts at outrageous prices.

NOT YOUR AVERAGE PET FOOD

Dog

So what does the flesh of man's best friend taste like? According to those who have tried it, the meat is chewy, somewhat fatty and similar to duck, goose or dark pork. While not the most common dish, especially as pet ownership becomes more widespread among affluent Asians, dog is nibbled on in many countries, including Korea and Vietnam. Often referred to as the "fragrant meat," it is relatively pricey, although older generations still believe various canine parts help increase energy and benefit health ailments. While the sight of skinned puppy carcasses in Asian street markets might send most of us screaming to the nearest McDonald's, we should take heart in the fact that virtually every part of the dog is used, even the fur (er, which one hopes isn't the fuzzy trim on those imported "Made in China" winter coats at the local mall).

In Korea, *bosintang* is a dog meat soup often eaten on very hot days. During the 1988 Olympics, its name was changed to one meaning "nutritious soup" so as not to offend westerners. Similar Scooby snacks were banned from Chinese restaurants during the 2008 Beijing Olympics. Perhaps in time, the fricasseed Fido trend will have rolled over to become a thing of the past.

In 2007, a British artist ate a corgi dog, Queen Elizabeth's favorite breed, to protest a fox hunt in which Prince Philip, the monarch's husband, had participated. The vegetarian artist said the dog (which had allegedly died of natural causes) was minced with apple, onion and seasoning but tasted "really, really disgusting."

Cat

Remove the head, skin, feet and tail, and cat carcass is a dead ringer for rabbit. Cat meat was euphemistically referred to as "roof rabbit" during times of famine. Urban legends (and some real cases) of stray feline passed off as hare or mutton abound, but it's unlikely that western society will accept a Fluffy flambé on the menu, no matter how flavorsome these felines may be. Kitty's relatives, such as civets (in the days before SARS), are considered a luxury dish, and in some countries, domesticated cats meow pitifully from their cages in crowded markets. They are usually scrawny strays, and people have become sick after eating cats that have ingested rat poison. The cats did get one good break during the 2008 Beijing Olympics, when the government ordered that no designated Olympic restaurants serve cat on their menus. And in Vietnam, selling cats for food became illegal when the rat population exploded and invaded rice crops. Hello, kitty, there is hope!

An empty stomach is not a good political adviser.
– Albert Einstein

Rat and Mouse

Don't recoil in disgust. While some of us keep these scurrying rodents as pets (and many more try to exterminate them from homes), the rat on some menus costs twice as much as beef. These unusual restaurants prefer to obtain country "mountain rats" as opposed to the city ones because they are (apparently) cleaner for recipes such as simmered mountain rat with black beans, mountain rat soup and mountain rat curry. Whether or not the rats were taken from fields, farms or a back alley is debatable, but delectable rat dishes turn up in many countries from India to South America and Africa. Once dispatched, the rodents are skinned and cut up into tiny pieces that can be passed off as nondescript chicken parts. For smaller appetites, grilled baby mice are dipped in a sauce and eaten whole, usually in one crispy bite.

Hedgehog

The *Larousse Gastronomique* describes boiled hedgehog as a popular 16th-century Parisian dish that tastes like wild rabbit. Hedgehog does not grace too many menus in modern times, partly because of its pet status and also because the quills are a pain to remove. Those medieval chefs, on the other hand, certainly knew how to cook these prickly rodents. First, the hedgehog was covered in wet clay, then roasted until its casing had completely hardened. When the clay came off, so did the quills, and what remained was a cooked, easy-to-skin, roast hedgehog.

Horse

During World War II, when the price of beef skyrocketed, horsemeat became a cheaper alternative for U.S. consumers. In Britain, meat rationing meant that die-hard horse lovers unwittingly sampled their divine equines in sausages and stews. As appalling as that might sound, horsemeat is occasionally eaten worldwide in countries such as France, China and South America. If you can afford it, even Japanese menus list *basashi*—cherry pink, thinly sliced, raw horseflesh. Why would anyone want to devour My Little Pony or put Black Beauty on a buffet table? Although forbidden by Jewish custom and in some other cultures, horsemeat is less fatty than beef, with a stronger, slightly sweet flavor. In Belgium, it is a preferred meat for steak tartare, and chefs laud its rich taste. But while early man hunted wild horses for food, and modern humans still cook it, most of us have reservations when it comes to eating equine meals, even if a galloping gourmet prepares them.

Guinea Pig

First of all, guinea pigs are not pigs. They are rodents—the beloved pets of thousands of children and the main meal of even more people. Domesticated as a food source since 5000 BC, the guinea pig, also known as a cavy or cuy, is a South American staple because it is compact and quick to reproduce. Guinea pig meat contains high amounts of protein and very little fat. That may not make the sight of one roasted and split lengthwise with its full head (including two buckteeth) on a plate more palatable for most of us, but many cultures love to eat their guinea pigs. In Peru, cavy food history is celebrated with festivals such as the *jaca tsariy*, or "collecting the cuys." Even certain churches in Lima depict the famous Last Supper painting with Jesus and the 12 disciples ready to eat a roast guinea pig. During the 16th century, invading Spaniards opposed this religious interpretation and tried to exterminate the guinea pig. Fearing rebellion, they stopped short, and today, guinea pigs remain a significant part of Peruvian tradition and cuisine, with some 65 million of these cuddly creatures devoured annually.

HUMAN CUISINE

If a new acquaintance admits he's into anthropopaghy, be afraid, very afraid. And whatever you do, please don't reply with "bite me." Anthropophagy, the scientific term for eating human flesh and commonly referred to as cannibalism, isn't exactly polite dinner conversation. Archaeological evidence, such as knife cuts on skulls and the discovery of preserved human waste containing a protein unique to the human heart muscle, allows us to infer that humans may have been practicing cannibalism for thousands of years. Ancient hunter-gatherers probably ate their dead friends and foes because, hey, they were fresh meat. The feeding frenzy likely stopped, not out of disgust for a "taboo" meat, but rather because farming and livestock domestication brought with it a sense of status. Once humans could afford, food-wise, to bury their dead, it became the thing to do.

Cannibalism didn't die out completely. Captured prisoners were killed and their flesh cooked, often to inflict the final insult. In other cultures, if an enemy had acted courageously before death, his heart was cut out and eaten so as to impart heroic qualities to the one who consumed it. Cannibalistic rituals may have prevailed in isolated communities. Members of one New Guinea tribe, who consumed various bits of deceased relatives during funeral rites, developed *kuru*, a fatal brain disease similar to "mad cow." And although they weren't considered food, Egyptian mummies (and perhaps even human organs or fetuses) were once ground into a powder and sold for their purported medicinal properties.

Then there is the stuff of horror films, the stories of famine and doomed journeys during which starved survivors chow down on each other, or psychopaths who can't get enough soul food. While rare (no pun intended), these instances are enough to send a chill down anyone's spine.

An American Cannibal, Allegedly

In 1873, Alfred (Alferd) Packer and five other mining prospectors became stranded in the Colorado Rocky Mountains during severe weather. Months later, only Packer returned and was subsequently jailed for murder. Although Packer claimed self-defense, evidence of cannibalism surfaced, and local media devoured the story. Initially sentenced to death, Packer was paroled in 1901 and is said to have become a vegetarian.

A Trail to Tragedy

The Donner Party was a group of settlers who became snowbound in the mountains of the Sierra Nevada. In the spring of 1846, over 80 emigrants led by a man named George Donner set out by wagon for a new life in California. They reached the mountains in mid-October and camped at two lakes, several miles apart. The harsh winter weather arrived early, and by December, the hungry group had run out of supplies. Desperate for food, they slaughtered all their animals and boiled the rawhide. About 15 members went to seek help at a fort about 100 miles away but became caught in a severe blizzard. When some of their group died, the others were tragically compelled to eat the bodies in order to survive. Two men and five women eventually made it to safety, and rescue parties were sent back to the camp. In total, 41 members of the ill-fated Donner Party perished in the ordeal.

Food is the most primitive form of comfort.
– Sheilah Graham, 1904–88

Windigo Possession

A Cree trapper named Swift Runner was executed in 1879 for killing and eating his family. Prior to the grisly incident, Swift Runner claimed to have suffered horrifying nightmares and irrational outbursts. He believed he was taken over by a windigo, a horrifying mythological creature in Native cultures that has a craving for human flesh. Windigo possession was likely a form of illness in which a starving or mentally disturbed person became cannibalistic.

Sunk, Stranded and Starving

Herman Melville's famous novel, *Moby Dick*, was inspired by the real-life shipwreck of the Massachusetts whaling ship, the *Essex*. In 1820, a sperm whale rammed the *Essex* until it sank in the Pacific, 2000 miles off the coast of South America. The 20 crewmembers managed to escape in small whaleboats and eventually reached a small, uninhabited island. They devoured all the birds, fish and vegetation they could find but soon realized the island could not sustain them.

All but three got back into the boats, and what happened next was more shocking than any work of fiction. One after another, the weakest sailors perished in the open boats. The corpses were initially thrown into the sea, but as days dragged on, the famished crew ate the flesh of anyone who died. When that food source ran out, they drew lots to select who would be shot and eaten. Ninety-three days after her sinking, the *Essex* survivors (including the three who had remained on the island) were rescued, but not before seven crewmembers had become dinner.

Notorious Killer

Milwaukee serial murderer Jeffrey Dahmer killed 17 men and boys, dismembered the bodies, ate their flesh and stored the remains in a freezer or acid-filled vats. Sentenced to life terms totaling almost 1000 years, Dahmer himself was murdered in prison in 1994.

Alive, But Barely

Friday, October 13, 1972, was an unlucky day for Flight 571 from Uruguay. The plane never arrived at its destination of Santiago, Chile, and instead crashed during bad weather in a snowy, remote region of the Andes Mountains. Miraculously, half of the initial 45 passengers survived, mostly young men who were members of a rugby team. They endured altitude sickness and freezing nights in a makeshift shelter built from the fuselage and had only a few chocolate bars and candies for food. Listening to a transistor radio, they learned the disheartening news that the search for them had been called off after 11 days. Shortly thereafter, an avalanche buried the wreckage and claimed eight more lives. The starving survivors resorted to "survival cannibalism" and ate the flesh of their already deceased companions while they waited for better weather conditions and a chance to seek help. After two months, three of the men took small pouches of "meat" for sustenance and trekked over the mountains. They were successful, and all the survivors were rescued a few days before Christmas. Today, a memorial marks the crash site.

> I do wish we could chat longer, but I'm having an old friend for dinner.
>
> – Hannibal Lecter (Anthony Hopkins), *Silence of the Lambs*

Placenta

Mother animals frequently eat the placenta after giving birth. It's a nutritious organ, full of vitamins and minerals, so why waste it? More than a few human mothers think the same way, and placentophagy (eating placenta) happens daily around the world. Various cultures practice it as part of the birth rite, and it is commonly believed that nutrients in the placenta assist the mother in recovering from childbirth and help prevent postpartum hemorrhages or depression.

The placenta can be used in any recipe that calls for beef or liver. Add cooked placenta pieces to tomato sauce and serve over pasta, or dehydrate the organ until it becomes a kind of placenta jerky and crumble over other foods. For those who can't stomach placenta, another option is to plant the leftover organ under, or along with, a tree and make Mother Nature proud.

CHAPTER 5

Leftovers

HEADY STUFF

Is eating brain a dumb idea? Do you have a problem tasting tongues? Does fried liver make you quiver? Are you unable to get past the "kidney" part in steak and kidney pie? If you answered yes to any of the above questions, you may have offal issues. You're not alone. Offal, the internal organs of slaughtered animals, has fallen out of favor in recent decades. Perhaps it's because we think of these "off-cuts," "variety meats" or "scrapple" as the parts swept off the butcher's floor after the choice sections have been sliced away. In reality, they are flavorsome pieces available at rock-bottom prices, no less. In past generations, no part of an animal was wasted, including the brain, bone marrow, kidneys, liver, testicles, heart, spleen, intestines, stomach...heck, throw in the head, feet and tail, as well. Offal is definitely not awful but rather the basis of time-honored traditions and nourishing meals like the kind Grandma used to make. Despite our aversion to ingesting innards, there is hope that these dishes will not fade into culinary oblivion. A few brave new chefs are being encouraged to look beyond the fillet and experiment again with "head to tail" cooking.

Head

Remember those pictures in elementary school medieval history books? A feast just wasn't a feast without a roast pig or boar head served on a silver platter. If you looked closely, you could even see two hard-boiled eggs in place of piggy eyeballs. Whole animal heads, usually pig, ox,

cow, sheep or lamb, have always been baked, boiled and smoked into nutritious, albeit unusual dishes around the world. The flesh stuck to the skull provides heaps of gelatinous meaty chunks. Calf's head, in particular, remains a classic in French cuisine and can be served hot or cold, stuffed, fried or garnished as a main entrée.

Unless you've been brought up on these particular foods, you may require a strong stomach to eat head. You probably need an even sturdier one to watch it being prepared. Apart from the scary sight of a flesh-covered cranium on the kitchen counter, the head needs to be boiled to separate the meat from the bone. The author of the 1829 *American Frugal Housewife* advises head cookers to "leave the windpipe on, for if it hangs out of the pot while the head is cooking, all the froth will escape through it." Fortunately, most heads today can be purchased already cut up so you don't have to play culinary chainsaw massacre.

Smalahove

This traditional Norwegian dish begins as a decapitated, brainless sheep's or lamb's head with a stake shoved through the nostrils. Next, it is held over a fire to burn off any remaining bits of wool and then smoked. Finally, the head is boiled for a few hours and served warm with vegetables. Not to be outdone, other cultures have their own versions of singed and boiled baa baa head, including the Icelandic *svie*, Mexico's *cabeza de cabrito* (goat's head with cooked brains) and Scottish sheep's head broth.

> Every part of a pig is edible, except the squeal.
> – Old culinary saying

Hog's Head Stew

This is one down-home stew to really pig out on. Raw pig's head can be purchased fairly inexpensively at local butcher shops, but don't forget to brush away the dirt from the pig's snout and teeth before cooking (evidently, pigs can get dirty). Boil it for as long as possible, then add spices and vegetables.

Head Cheese

Head cheese is *sooo* not a cheese. This jellied lunchmeat does not contain an ounce of dairy product. It is made from the boiled head of a pig or a calf, occasionally a sheep or cow, and often the feet, tongue and heart, too. Also known as "brawn" in England, or "souse" when pickled with vinegar, and *picti* in Greece, head cheese can be a sausage or a jellied loaf. To make it, the eyeballs are removed, the ears cleaned out and the head simmered for about five hours in seasoned water until the meat falls off. After the skull is removed, the cooked liquid can be strained and added to the meat. The chunky mixture is then poured into a mold and cooled in the refrigerator.

 76

Head cheese quickly turns into a jelly because of the natural gelatin in animal skulls. Once set, quickly slice through the jiggly form and serve as a luncheon meat. Call it a fancy cold cut and use it in school lunch sandwiches the next day.

Brains

Did You Know?

The ancient Romans picked through pig livers and entrails to predict the future.

In restaurants from Austria to Indiana, fried cow brain sandwiches are a hot lunchtime favorite. In Asia, local delicacies include simmered brains drenched in coconut cream or roasted calf brains wrapped in banana leaves. India has its brain curry, while in California, *sesos* is a cow brain taco filling. Grilled gray matter may give some a headache, but brain eating goes back centuries. The *Apicius* cookbook included a recipe for brains with rose petal, and one Roman emperor, Heliogablus, reputedly ordered 600 ostrich brains for an extravagant banquet. Lamb's brain is reputedly the finest type, but all brains require lengthy soaks in cold water as preparation. The organ's blood vessels and membranes must also be cut out, autopsy fashion, before it can be cooked. While cow's brain brunches are far from becoming ancient history, many jurisdictions have banned butchered brains from bovines over two years old for fear of "mad cow" disease, and some stores now only sell pork brains instead. Those worries didn't stop one American restaurant from hosting a cow-brain-eating contest. The winner ate over 17 pounds of this specialty meat in 15 minutes, and you could perhaps say he had more brawn than brains.

Monkey Brains

There's a rumor circulating on websites and in tabloid papers that the brains of live monkeys are eaten in secret restaurants throughout Asia or Africa. Apparently, the unfortunate simian is doped up with alcohol so as to make it virtually unconscious before its skull is opened to reveal a pulsating brain. Hungry, and obviously non-squeamish, diners then spoon out bits of the live monkey's brain and eat it. Although monkey has always been part of traditional medicine, and monkey meat is still sold as food, the practice of eating live monkey brains is likely an urban legend started by a foreign journalist in 1948. Unfortunately, the story still pops up in the media, likely perpetuated by bored Internet bloggers suffering from years of undiagnosed Big Mac attacks.

> Ah, dessert! Chilled monkey brains.
> – from *Indiana Jones and the Temple of Doom* (1984)

Neck

Animal neck, when used with part of the shoulder and rib, is called "scrag." Perhaps it's no coincidence that the neck as a body part on any creature often looks rather "scraggy" (especially the ones right below a Beverly Hills face-lift). As an animal meat, gristly scrag should be cooked slowly, and you should save fatty pork neck for sausage only. When it comes to turkey necks (not the plastic surgery kind), this mystery poultry part is usually included with the giblets. Certain regions of France specialize in not-too-shabby dishes that include stuffed neck of duck or goose.

Tongue

Cow tongue on white with a touch of lettuce and Dijon mustard? Now that's a drool-worthy sandwich. This common cold cut is found in delis around the world, and any tongue—if you can get away from the yuck factor—is edible. Larger tongues, such as those of beef or oxen, are meaty enough to be stuffed with *foie gras* and truffles. Braised calf tongue is a common European entrée, and lamb tongue, reputedly the most delicate, sells for about five dollars a can in New Zealand. In northern climates, jellied or smoked caribou (also called reindeer) tongue is touted as a "kingdom of the midnight sun" specialty. So don't stick out your tongue when offered this offal. Whether pickled, sliced, boiled or simmered, much of the world thinks of this fleshy organ as a juicy treat that simply slips between the lips.

Did You Know?

Pink flamingo tongue was served as a delicacy in ancient Rome, while blackbird tongue was popular during the Middle Ages.

Facial Parts

Let's face it, pigs, sheep, cows and goats—they all include some tasty facial parts. In Ireland, you can order a dish that is essentially a pig's face with cabbage, and in the Middle East, there's *pacha*, the skinned and boiled face of a sheep or goat. Order a *taco de cabeza* in a Mexican restaurant, but be forewarned; the meat is from the cow's head (*de lengua* is from its tongue, and *sesos* is cow brains). Pig's snout, however, truly does scrape the bottom of the pork barrel. These honkers are really only suitable as a sausage meat (can you say "hot dog"?) but other porcine parts make surprisingly good eats. Breaded or grilled ears or curly pig's tails are the ultimate in chewy hors d'oeuvres, sort of like a classy pork rind. To eat the eyeball of virtually any animal, pierce it first with a tiny bite so the jelly squirts out. Next, chew well, preferably with your molars, and savor every oozing ounce. Seal eyeballs are a special Inuit treat, the equivalent of one of those candies with the exploding juicy center.

Pig's Face and Cabbage

Cut the meat from one side of a pig's head in one piece.

Soak it in cold water overnight and boil it (15 minutes per pound) with a head of cabbage.

Score the skin and bake the face, skin side up, at 350°F until the cracklings are crisp and well browned.

Chop the drained cabbage and arrange on a platter about the face. Serve with a sauce made from the pan drippings.

(Reprinted with permission from WildRecipes.com.)

Cow Lips

Indonesia possesses many exotic delights, including *rujak cingur*, a traditional East Java dish made of mixed vegetables and cow lips. More correctly, the lips in rujak cingur come from a certain part of the cow's snout, not the mashed up, barely hot-dog legal stuff. Rujak cingur is covered in a seasoned sauce, which includes black shrimp paste, peanuts, chili and cucumber juice. Foreigners flock to the many local vendors who sell plates of the delicacy, but most of the locals don't tell them about the cow lip part.

Hog Jowl

Down south, this is the cubed, cured and smoked cheek, or jowl, of a hog used to flavor stews. Hog jowls can also be fried up like bacon, but make sure they're well wrapped in the refrigerator or everything in it will smell like, well, pieces of Porky's face. As British fare, pig cheeks, plus half the jawbone and tongue, are coated in breadcrumbs and known as "chaps." In the U.S., five million pounds of jowls are sold every year, particularly in December, when wolfing down these greasy cuts on New Year's Day, along with black-eyed peas and collard greens, is believed to bring good luck.

Did You Know?

The longest word in a literary work is from an ancient Greek comedy of the fourth century BC and describes a fricassee dish with 17 ingredients, including fish, shark, pigeon, honey, scraps and wine: Lopadotemachoselachogaleokranioleipsanodrimhypotrimmatosilphioparaomelitokatakechymenokichlepikossyphophattoperisteralektryonoptekephalliokigklopeleiolagoiosiraiobaphetraganopterygon (182 letters). Now, that's a mouthful!

BITS and BITES

Heart

If you want a fat-free meat, eat your heart out with this organ. Heart, a type of red offal (and it should be bright red when purchased, not brown, blue or any other color), contains no fat and, like most organ meats, is highly nutritious. Flavorful calf's heart can be stuffed, roasted or sautéed. It can also be cubed, chicken-heart size, and grilled on skewers.

Kidney

When eating kidney, try not to think about its previous function. Yes, this organ purified the animal's blood, and yes, it "made pee pee," but kidney has a unique, interesting flavor. Don't stare at its smooth surface and wonder if yours looks similar. Simply enjoy it cooked in such time-honored cuisine as calf's kidney brochettes, lamb's kidneys à l'anglaise or the pub favorite, steak and kidney pie. Enjoy and wash it down with a cold draft to help your kidneys get back to work.

Melt, Elder, Lights and Bladders

Some meats sound tempting, but be careful what you buy, as culinary words can cause confusion. If a recipe calls for "melt," this is another term for the spleen (a common sausage meat), "elder" is a cow's udder (mostly shuddered at these days) and "lights" is a medieval word meaning lungs. Slaughtered animal lungs aren't that heavy, either, and British fare includes this inexpensive meat in "liver and lights," fried up with onions. According to the *Larousse Gastronomique*, lungs must be first "beaten to expel the air." The culinary encyclopedia also describes the way poultry can be stuffed into a pig's bladder and poached, since "this cooking method, in which the bird is effectively sealed, concentrates the flavors."

Tripe

There's a whitish, densely textured substance in the meat section. What is it and why is it so cheap? The word "tripe" often refers to garbage, rubbish or something worthless, but as a food, tripe is the tissue lining of a ruminant's (usually a cow's or sheep's) stomach. Tripe can also be purchased pickled or canned. Don't buy any tripe with a green or brown tinge (unless it's for the pooch), and wash fresh tripe well before cooking. It soaks up the flavor of broth or sauces and a variety of dishes. People around the world can stomach tripe. How about you?

Besides the always-popular tripe soup, international tripe dishes include:

Tripes à la Caen: a gourmet French tripe dish

Chakna: a spicy goat tripe stew served in India

Tripe and onions: a traditional British dish

Buche: pork tripe in Mexican tacos

Fried tripe: battered in cornmeal then dipped in blistering oil and served in the U.S.

Menudo: Mexican cow stomach soup, thought to cure hangovers

Hot Dogs

Beloved in ballparks, arenas, picnics and from street vendors, hot dogs are as American as apple pie, with at least 20 billion chowed down on each year. But have you ever bitten into a nice, warm hot dog, or corn dog, only to feel a tiny, gritty object crunch between your molars? Is it, could it be, a piece of bone? Don't be surprised—this is, after all, a food that bears no resemblance to its former existence. One ingredient found in many hot dogs is "mechanically separated meat." Picture it now: bones with meat chunks still clinging to them (known as "attached edible meat") shoved through a sieve-type instrument to remove the meat. Out it comes as a meaty paste that makes baby food in a jar look like haute cuisine. Inevitably, minute bits of bone pass through this robot butcher, hence the gritty feeling when you chomp down. Although the government banned mechanically separated beef in 2004 because of fears over mad cow disease, the process is still used for pork, chicken and turkey, along with "advanced meat recovery" systems designed to remove meat from the bone and prevent a few human fingers from ending up in your mouth, too. Hot dogs can also be made from "variety meats" or "meat by-products," euphemisms for liver, kidney or heart and various other parts you wouldn't otherwise purchase. Best bet? Check the label. Buy hot dogs listed as all beef, all chicken or all pork, and watch out for that mysterious "may contain..." phrase.

Andouille

This spiced and smoked pork sausage is chock full of the gastrointestinal system of pigs. One type is even made with smaller intestines placed into larger ones—a sort of stack 'em guts. When served cold or grilled, whiffs of a manure-like smell surround these fine French sausages. The diner is reminded that, after all, andouille is made from the stomach and colon. A cleaned and cooked colon, yes, but in some phantom fashion, the smell of its former contents still lingers.

Haggis

The very word "haggis" is enough to turn most stomachs inside out. Take a sheep's heart, liver and lungs, mix with oatmeal, onion and spices, and boil together. Stuff the mixture into the sheep's stomach (a casing is often used nowadays), but poke a few holes in it before heating because there is nothing worse than exploded sheep guts all over the kitchen. Similar offal-stuffed stomach cuisine exists in many other regions—stuffed hog maw is one American example—but Scottish haggis has a fan base like no other. For one, it has its own special day, January 25, or Robert Burns Day. Burns, an 18th-century Scot, wrote "Address to a Haggis," a poem still recited amid pomp and bagpipes, and at the center of attention, a haggis, is paraded. Then there is haggis hurling, a cross

between a sport and a controlled food fight. The world-record holder flung his 1-1/2-pound haggis a distance of 180 feet. If you do try this famous dish, some recommend a small glass of straight Scotch poured over your serving of haggis. If that doesn't help the taste, you could always exercise your throwing arm.

Chitterlings

The roots of this southern U.S. food date back to when African American slaves were given only the unwanted hog parts, such as the ears, feet and innards, and forced to make their meals out of these scraps. Chitterlings, also known as chitlins, are cooked pig intestines. Like all piggy parts, they must be cleaned properly and simmered for a few hours for best results. One town in South Carolina holds an annual event, the Chitlin' Strut, during which over 128,000 pounds of chitterlings are eaten by 70,000 hungry festival-goers.

Liver Pâté

Have a hunk of pâté, the putty-like food made from mashed meat and fat. For over 5000 years, the livers of poultry, fish or pork have been minced into this thick spread. Liverwurst, a German pork liver pâté, is often served on toast with sliced pickles to children. Goose (and sometimes duck) liver pâté, or *foie gras* in French, is perhaps the most famous and controversial. The reason? Gavage, a process even the Romans used, in which geese are force-fed for a few weeks before slaughter in order to fatten their livers. Animal rights activists argue that shoving a feeding tube down a goose's throat is cruel; *foie gras* advocates say it only sounds uncomfortable, and mother ducks force-feed their goslings in a similar manner with their beaks. The method is so controversial that certain cities have even banned *foie gras*.

Moose Muffle

This isn't a fashionable hand warmer but rather another term for a moose's nose. The muffle, or mouffle, is the flappy, pendulous lippy overhang of this big-game mammal. Early Aboriginal peoples considered this part of the moose snout a delicacy, although today's trophy hunters might not want to ruin their prized moose head for a moose muffle sandwich. Boiled, baked, fried or jellied, it is recommended that any large, bristly hairs, or moose mustache, be removed before cooking. It takes one or two muffles plus a couple of onions to make a good broth or stew. Cut up the muffles first, and no one will recognize a massive floating lip in the soup.

Lard

In the world of fats and oils, lard badly needs a marketing makeover. This rendered pig fat contains huge amounts of vitamin D and only 40 percent saturated fat compared with almost 60 percent for butter. Plain and simple, lard is very greasy, just like the stuff left behind in the skillet after the morning's bacon is cooked. The *crème de la crème* of this greasy goop is leaf lard, direct from the hard fat around a pig's kidneys. Backfat, from the pig's back, is a more readily available substitute. Both these lards are indispensable ingredients in old-fashioned cooking and baking. Sure, the hydrogenated commercial stuff has the reputation of being a trans-fat, cholesterol-laden clogger ready to choke the life out of your arteries, but there is nothing quite like good-quality, additive-free lard. In Germany, lard is served with cracklings (fried pig skin) or as a spread on bread, and a chicken or goose fat called *schmaltz* is frequently used in Jewish cooking. Lard makes the flakiest pie crusts, crispiest deep-fried chicken and French fries to die for. Oh, lard help us all.

Did You Know?

Long before plastic tubs existed, dried pigs' bladders were used as containers for tallow and lard.

PRIVATE PARTS

Animelles

Also called lamb fries in Italy, *animelles de moutons frites* in France and *criadillas* in Spain, these are the testicles of young rams and, occasionally, bull calves. The *Larousse Gastronomique* refers to them (and oysters—the seafood, not the prairie kind) as an aphrodisiac but warns they are "less agreeable to delicate people with feeble stomachs." No kidding—these are sheep's balls we're talking about, not chopped liver. Culinary cookbooks often refer to animal testicles as "white kidneys" because they can be cooked like kidneys. Animelles may be served skinned, cut into pieces and then fried, or battered in a flour-and-beer mixture. To firm them up, marinate them first in onions and stock, then roll them in breadcrumbs and serve with parsley. And if you visit Iceland, try them pickled.

Prairie Oysters

No, these are not shellfish found in the middle of a corn-field. Prairie or Rocky Mountain oysters are bull (and sometimes buffalo, sheep or prairie dog) testicles. That's right, these are the leftovers from bovine castration, also called calf fries, cowboy caviar, tendergroins and swing-ing beef. Once deveined and cleaned, these membranous blobs can be breaded, deep-fried, sautéed, braised or poached. Although gulping down a large male animal's family jewels won't elevate the diner's testosterone level one microgram, that hasn't stopped various "testicle festivals" from growing in popularity in cowboy towns such as Clinton, Montana.

Penis

Some people just don't get it. Ingesting male animal organs does not increase the consumer's testosterone or virility (for that, you need a doctor's prescription). Nevertheless, sliced or diced penises still appear on menus throughout Asia. They're also available shriveled up and dried in health-food stores. These include, but are not limited to, ox, deer, goat, horse, donkey and even tiger or seal penis. Also available are bottles of alcohol or rice wine in which bits of preserved deer or other animal penises float. Certain restaurants even offer a combination of more than one as a tonic (how about a cow, pig and turtle penis cocktail?). As long as there is demand, penis remains available. The truth is often hard to swallow.

Rectum and Uterus

Let's get to the bottom of whether or not animal rectums can be eaten. Like any mammalian organs, they are edible, but not exactly everyday eats. Those who truly want to masticate these thick, rubbery, former manure tubes are usually limited to money-hungry contestants on gross-out game shows. Still, it is possible to ask for "bung" at the local butcher shop and not be met with shocked stares. Bung is another term for pig rectum, and if you look hard enough, you can find bull rectum and testicle soup on Asian menus. Stuffed pig uterus may be slightly more common. Steaming pig uterus is ordinarily available throughout Indochina, sliced into little coils and ready to be dipped into hot chili sauce. Don't be shocked—it's not an outrageous new fad. Even the ancient Romans gobbled down pig uterus sausage and cooked sow udders stuffed with sea urchin gonads in a puff-pastry pie. Yum.

TENDER TOOTSIES

Pig's Feet

Unlike sheep's or lamb's trotters, you don't have to worry about woolly tufts in between pig's toes. If you can get past their amputated appearance, pig's trotters, the feet and often the pig's knuckles, contain tasty strands of meat. They can be cooked in almost any way imaginable—barbecued, boiled, pickled or coated with egg and breadcrumbs and grilled. One Italian specialty is *zampone* (which means "large trotter") and consists of a pig's foot stuffed with ground pork, bacon, truffles and seasoning, and then smoked and boiled. Legend has it this dish was invented during the siege of an Italian city. The starving inhabitants did not want to leave anything to the invaders, not even their pigs' feet, so they invented a specialty dish out of the leftovers. Zampone is often served at New Year's along with a side dish of lentils. The lentils symbolize the coins to be earned during the coming year, while the pig's foot represents the purse. The Irish also love pig's trotters as boiled "crubeens," which probably makes them the only feet eaten as a finger food.

Camel's Feet

Move over piggies, camels are the new tasty trotters, and we're not talking about a brand of cigarettes. While these desert workhorses don't have cloven hooves (as in, not kosher) camel is eaten in the Middle East, Mongolia and Africa, and is even farmed in Australia. No doubt barbecued or pickled camel's feet make some fearless diners kick up their heels. Aristotle wrote of eating grilled camel's feet, and the *Larousse Gastronomique* includes a recipe for camel's feet *à la vinaigrette*.

Chicken and Duck Feet

One day you may be able to walk into a fast-food joint and order a combo platter of breaded chicken feet and fried duck webs. Sure, these scrawny talons and webbed walkers look odd, but so did chicken wings before they became *über* trendy. Millions around the world already snack on these savory feet, plus a chicken's claw comes in handy as a toothpick. Asian restaurants often serve them rolled in black bean sauce, and Chinese dim sum usually includes chicken feet, known as "phoenix talons," on the menu. In South Africa, the cooked feet are referred to as "chicken dust," so dubbed after a favorite chicken pastime—scratching around in the dirt. Poultry feet also make an excellent soup stock, but be sure to clean them well before use—you never know (or maybe you do) what they've stepped in.

Cow's Feet

As with hooves, trotters and other animal feet, cow's and calves' feet fall into that "white offal" or "variety meat" category (once again, the ubiquitous hot dog ingredient). Butchers usually sell them already blanched and cleaned, though most are boiled so the gelatin leaches out to thicken stock and other broths. Cook them for at least two hours, then remove the bones and season to taste. Calves' feet may be cooked the same way as a calf's head. The feet can also be jellied, breaded or grilled separately for some tasty toe jam.

Seal Flipper

Seal meat has always been a staple for Inuit hunters. Every part of the seal can be consumed, including its pink, fatty blubber and that juicy treat, raw seal eyeball. Many a Maritime tourist has enjoyed Newfoundland's seal flipper pie. Seal flipper is actually the shoulder of the seal rather than its paw, but shoulder pie just didn't have the same ring to it.

CHAPTER 6

Bloody Awful

BOILED BLOOD

One basic fact about blood: it congeals. This useful property has made blood one of the most user-friendly and nutritious culinary ingredients for thousands of years. Pour some of this dark red liquid into any vegetable or meat broth as an instant thickener. While certain religions such as Judaism prohibit mixing food with blood, this vital fluid frequently turns up in international cuisine. In Asia, congealed animal and poultry blood is sold in jellied, tofu-like squares for use in soup, or as a separate meal on a plate with crackers. Tibetans eat a congealed yak's blood dish called *ragati*, and blood-based patties are as close as your nearest ethnic groceteria. Some tribes, such as the Maasai, gently bleed their livestock for a convenient or ceremonial beverage. The blood is drunk fresh, boiled or mixed with yogurt. Throw in a celery stick and you could call it the original Bloody Caesar.

BLOODY AWFUL

Blood Stew

A common Filipino blood stew, dinuguan, is nicknamed "chocolate pudding" because of its rich brown color. Spiced with lemongrass, this thick saucy mixture of pork and pig's blood doesn't taste like blood at all, but rather a robust, mouthwatering blend of meats and seasonings. Vampires may be disappointed.

Blood Sausage

Homer's *Odyssey* mentions a full stomach "filled with blood and fat." Add fillers such as fat, bread, barley, rice or oatmeal, stuff everything into a pig's intestine and, presto, blood sausage. Frequently served in Europe, this traditional food is internationally renowned under assorted names, such as the German *blutwurst* (with bacon and lungs), the Italian *sanguinaccio* (pig's brains optional), the Spanish *morcillia* or *butifarras* and the French *boudins noirs* (spiked with brandy). In the UK, blood sausage is known as black pudding. Served fried along with white pudding (a fatty sausage without blood), grilled tomatoes, potatoes and soda bread, it's the breakfast of champions. A pub in the United Kingdom even hosts the World Black Pudding Throwing Contest. Legend has it that the event is based on a battle in which both armies were said to have run out of ammunition so they threw food at each other.

Trivia Tidbit

In 2005, a British dairy unveiled its black pudding ice cream at a local festival. The frosty dessert contained bits of black pudding similar to the chips in chocolate chip ice cream.

Snake's Blood

The following shooter is not for the squeamish, though it is straight from the heart, literally. Grass snakes in Vietnam and other Asian countries are slit open in front of the customer, and the blood is drained into a glass of rice wine. The snake's heart is quickly removed and plopped into a shot glass. The bloody wine mixture is then poured over the still-beating heart, and the whole concoction immediately gulped down by the willing guest. Often the bile is also squeezed from the gallbladder into a separate glass. This greenish liquid chaser supposedly reduces phlegm and coughs. How much should one expect to pay for this gory guzzler? In some countries, such as Indonesia, a king cobra snake blood shot can set you back $100, while the black and white cobra is a steal at only $10. Cheers!

Did You Know?

Vampires and mosquitoes aren't the only ones interested in a sanguine supper. Other species, besides bedbugs and other insects that exist entirely on blood, include the vampire bat and vampire finches in the Galapagos. An inch-long relative of the catfish also darts into a host fish's gills, sucks up a blood dinner, then leaves to find the next brunch, and a type of starling called the oxpecker picks bugs off rhinos, giraffes and other large animals but also nips a blood snack at the same time.

Blood Dumplings

These northern European and Scandinavian dumplings can be made from the blood of any animal, even that of reindeer. They're easier to make than blood sausages because no stuffing or sausage casings are required. Blood dumplings are basically a mixture of flour, blood, onion and spices dropped into boiling water for several minutes. While these lumpy dough balls vaguely resemble recently excised cancerous growths, they're a hot and satisfying alternative to pasta or bread. Eat them immediately or fry them up and serve them with potatoes and lingonberry sauce.

> The belly rules the mind.
> – Spanish proverb

RAW MEAT

Steak Tartare

Some like it raw, and the *crème de la crème* of uncooked meat is steak tartare. Order this gourmet food, and you'll likely be introduced to a very thin slice of steak or, more often, a chopped, minced pile of lean, raw beef (or horsemeat) topped with seasonings and the orangy orb of an uncooked egg yolk. If fresh flesh is *de rigeur* for you, steak tartare is as raw as it gets. Do not send it back to the kitchen with complaints of it being underdone—you'll only insult the chef. Legend has it that "tartare" was named after the Tartar peoples of Europe and Asia, who were said to tenderize beef chunks by placing them in pouches under their saddles—an early type of food preparation multi-tasking, no doubt.

Meat Juices

What would a Sunday roast beef dinner be without gravy? Slop it over mashed potatoes, hot turkey sandwiches, even French fries, and it instantly turns any dish into comfort food. Just remember, real gravy is made from the boiled meat juices, a polite term for blood and lymph. Of course, that fact isn't something one wants to think about, especially during Thanksgiving dinner.

Marrow

Inside that cooked Sunday roast bone is a greasy, dark and salty substance some people love to pick out and nibble. It's marrow, a tissue found in the cavities of the long bones where blood cells are produced. Marrow adds flavor to soups and stews, but many like to spread this savory substance on toast or canapés. Native peoples often ate it from a freshly killed moose for its protein value and energy-laden fat (unsaturated, no less).

Trivia Tidbit

Marrow is also the name of a type of pea and a squash.

Pia

The markets of Laos, Thailand and surrounding countries sell hundreds of peculiar foods, but one product stands out as particularly curious. What is that dark green-brown fluid sloshing around in those clear plastic bags? It doesn't look anything you'd want to drink, but it is sold right beside the foodstuffs. This unappealing swill, called *pia* or *khi phia*, comes from the stomach of a cow or water buffalo. It's not blood, but rather chyme, the partially digested watery leftovers of whatever the animal ate. Like any meal, the resulting substance would have eventually been processed into blood or, alternately, exited one end or another in the form of either excrement or vomit. Instead, pia is drained from the cow's duodenum after slaughter—a bovine last meal that usually resembles (and smells like) liquefied grass. Boiled and diluted pia adds flavor to cooking and is often used as a type of extreme dressing drizzled over spiced salads.

CHAPTER 7

Something Fishy Goin' On

SURF 'n' TURF IT

A seafood smorgasbord lurks beneath our planet's watery expanses. Oceans, lakes, rivers, even trickling streams host a plethora of living things. Thank heavens, or more correctly thank the seas, most of these creatures, no matter how baffling or hideous, are edible. Countless fish and fish-related products are consumed on a daily basis, and some 200 million people worldwide rely on fish for employment. From the average pan-fry to chewy blubber to spiny bottom-feeders, if you can catch it, you can probably eat it. It's good stuff, too. Seafood contains valuable nutrients often hard to come by in traditional landlubber grub, including omega-3 fatty acids and iodine. Will the seafood harvest always be there for humanity? According to one marine conservation society, 70 percent of the world's fish stocks are fully fished, overfished or depleted. Although one-third of seafood worldwide is produced by fish farms, and organic fisheries are booming, no fishy bite should be taken for granted. Ancient shell leftovers found in caves on South African beaches prove that early man ate shellfish at least 164,000 years ago. The love of seafood is as old as, well, dinnertime.

Jellyfish

See those slippery strips on your exotic Asian salad? They used to be *Cato stylus mosaicus* or one of many other species of edible jellyfish. Don't knock these brainless, faceless blobs. To their credit, these invertebrates

have been bobbing around the oceans for millions of years. A live, floating jellyfish is over 95 percent water, which explains why it tastes much like a wet, deflated balloon. The most edible parts include the round bulk of the jellyfish, called the umbrella or bell. Sliced or shredded, it adds a gelatinous consistency to cold salads, but jellyfish tends to be rather bland and needs a flavorful sauce. When sold dried or salted, jellyfish need to be soaked in water overnight before being made into moonlit sesame jellyfish and other wistfully named Asian dishes. Dried jellyfish can be ground into a powder used to make jellyfish tofu and cookies. In Malaysia, jellyfish are called "music to the teeth" because of the way their rubbery texture scrunches in your mouth.

Did You Know?

A sea turtle can't tell the difference between a jellyfish and a plastic bag. It unfortunately often ends up eating the latter and dies.

Skates and Rays

Is it a bird? A plane? How about a winter ice sport or a Florida baseball team? There are about 500 different kinds of skates and rays. These are flatfish with large fins and long tails—the stingray, electric ray, butterfly ray, manta ray, guitarfish and sawfish, to name a few. Like sharks, both skates and rays have cartilage and a viscous coating that can give them an ammonia smell if not washed properly. Skates are egg bearing and harmless, but watch out for the ray's stinger. Often bigger than skates, rays give birth to live young, which can make some species more prone to being on the endangered species list. The wings (fins) of both fish are usually sold ready-skinned and can be barbecued, fried or grilled and served with hollandaise or tomato sauce. When its pinkish tinge becomes white and flaky, this fibrous, light, sweet fish meat is ready for takeoff.

> Fish should smell like the ocean. If they smell like fish, it's too late.
>
> – Unknown

Stinkheads

Alaska's rotten fish head tradition certainly lives up to its name. During the first run of salmon, native Yup'ik villagers catch a netful of stinkhead fish, cut off the heads and bury the bodies in the ground. A month later the shriveled fish remains are dug up and eaten as a chewy treat. In the past, wooden barrels contained the heads and fish, but nowadays, plastic bags and buckets have replaced the barrels. The stinkhead custom likely developed as a way to preserve fish parts, not because everyone thought it would taste great. Funny how human taste can adapt, but for first-time stinker-eaters, this specialty is a surefire way to make your insides rumble. Some say stinkheads contain hallucinogenic properties, but when it comes to scoffing down putrefied fish heads, that's probably the only bonus.

stew-worthy variety is kombu, from the giant Pacific kelp, which can grow to lengths of 200 feet. If you live along the seaside regions of the United Kingdom, gather laver, a purplish seaweed found on the rocky shores. Boil it into a jelly, mix with oatmeal and cook it up as a patty called laver bread—comfort food and sea vegetable all in one.

Strange But Edible Sea Greens
(Okay, some are brown or red)

Bladder wrack (also called the sea oak, rockweed or rock wrack)
Dead man's fingers (sea sacs)
Sea parsley (dulse)
Sea lettuce
Sea otter's cabbage
Sea spaghetti
Winged kelp

Hairy Crab

Both the male and female hairy crab are about as fashionable as crabs get. Formerly called mitten crabs, these smallish, gray arthropods sport stiff, white, spiked hairs on their legs and fuzz on their claws that resemble old-fashioned fur muffs. Commonly farmed in fresh water, they're fattest in mid-October when they're ready to mate. Speaking of which, hairy crab ova is a favorite Shanghai dish. Even a recent G8 summit of world leaders had hairy crab bisque on the menu. Of course, no "hairs" were actually in the soup.

Did You Know?

Fancy a few steamed king crab legs? Then grab a ton of mayonnaise because there are five pairs on every crab, and the largest crabs measure five to eight feet across.

Crayfish

With buggy eyes and wavy antennae, crayfish (also called crawfish) are mini lobster replicas, except that they live in freshwater rivers and swamps or are farmed in ponds, especially in Louisiana. Sweden is the largest importer of American crayfish, and a blue-green Australian variety is called the yabby. The tail is the best part, but if their appearance is too creepy for you, crayfish can always be used as bait.

Dolphin

For many, it's a shame to think that these intelligent mammals could end up on someone's fork, but thousands are killed yearly for their meat. In Japan, dolphin is cheaper than whale and is often illegally passed off as such. As well, the "drive-hunt," a 400-year-old tradition in which a pod of dolphins is scared into a shallow bay for slaughter, draws worldwide condemnation. Ironically, dolphin meat (raw or canned) contains alarmingly high levels of mercury and chemical pollutants such as PCBs. Chalk it up as another good reason not to eat Flipper.

Maktaaq

Chewy and long lasting, with a hint of hazelnut flavor. If this sounds like the perfect chewing gum, go ahead, masticate away. *Maktaaq* (pronounced "muktuk") will give even the strongest jaws a workout, though you'll have to forgo the minty-fresh breath. It's the raw, black, outer skin layer of a whale, with about an inch of rubbery blubber included underneath. Inuit whale hunters of the 19th and 20th centuries prized young bowhead whale maktaaq eaten fresh after the kill, and narwhal or beluga maktaaq can still be bought for a few dollars a pound in Inuit co-op stores. High in protein, maktaaq may also be fried like bacon. Store slabs of this northern sushi in the Arctic's convenient refrigeration system—snow.

Whale Meat

Thar she blows, and it's not a fish, it's a mammal. Surprisingly, whale meat looks and tastes like beef. Despite an international moratorium on commercial whaling, Japan still hunts hundreds per year, mostly under the guise of scientific research. The whale meat actually ends up in markets and restaurants, and some Japanese restaurants serve expensive whale burgers, made with a deep-fried filling of minke whale, or raw whale sushi.

Body Sushi

Come up and see some *nyotaimori*, sometime. That's Japanese for body or naked sushi, as in a beautiful, unclothed woman lies on a table covered in a veritable sushi buffet. While this may verge on cuisine porn, it should be added for clarification that the perfect bodies under these California rolls aren't completely nude—they wear the skimpiest of bikinis. This naked sushi is the latest rage in California. Just watch where you put those chopsticks.

Eels

Slimy and squiggly eels were once part of Native and set-tler diets. Today, they've become a hard sell in the U.S. and Canada. With their serpent-like, muscular bodies, these electric fish also go by the name of water snakes and look downright creepy. Too bad, because eel has a delicate taste similar to turtle or chicken and is full of those beneficial omega-3 fatty acids. Traditionally caught at night, eels and their babies, called elvers, are best kept alive until just before cooking. The eel's thick skin peels off easily, and the succulent, firm flesh can be fried, baked into eel pie, grilled, stewed, smoked or even eaten raw as Japanese eel sushi and Britain's favorite, jellied eel. Eel has always been popular in Europe and Asia. In fact, a recent restoration of Leonardo da Vinci's famous painting, *The Last Supper*, shows a plate of eel and sliced oranges in front of Jesus and his apostles. Yes, if Jesus ate eels (according to da Vinci, anyway), so could you.

Foodie Fact

To get rid of a fishy smell on your fingers, rub your hands with salt and lemon juice.

Fugu

Forget suicide chicken wings, hellfire chili or biting the heads off live cockroaches. The Japanese fugu fish is the extreme of "eat-this-and-you-may-die" cuisine. This species of blowfish, or puffer fish, contains a chemical in its organs that is over 12,000 times deadlier than cyanide. If not prepared properly, ingesting fugu leaves you paralyzed—a sort of "living death"—for several hours until every muscle in your body, including your lungs, finally gives up. This fish is definitely licensed to kill, and there's no antidote. Estimates are that between 20 and 100 people die every year from fugu poisoning. It is also the one meal the Japanese emperor is not allowed to eat. Chefs wishing to serve fugu must first study for two years, and then pass strict exams, which more than half fail. Despite its potentially lethal side effects and exorbitant expense (a full fugu meal can cost between $200 and $1000), diners flock to fugu like the proverbial lemmings to a cliff. Among the few countries that legally serve fugu is the U.S., but importation is restricted to one supplier and one point of entry (JFK International Airport in New York). If you do decide to try fugu, don't be surprised if your lips and tongue go numb after the first bite. The best chefs intentionally leave a trace of poison for the diner's excitement. Then again, your chef may have been a slow learner or previous flunkie. Oh well, one way or another, you'll find out.

Candlefish

During the next blackout, try threading a wick through a dried fish and then light it like a candle. It's possible with the eulachon, or oolichan, a smelt-like fish of the Pacific Coast. One 19th-century writer referred to this little candlefish as being "so full of oil that it can be lighted at one end and used as a candle." The eulachon contains a grease similar in composition to olive oil and high in monounsaturates. Coastal peoples traded it as part of the historic "grease trails," and Native healers used it to treat skin conditions. Because the eulachon was an important food source until salmon came into season, it was also referred to as the "savior fish." Today, the name might be reserved for those who can't locate batteries for the emergency flashlight.

Catfish

There's no doubt about it, the catfish is one ugly catch. For one, there's the sticky, black, scaleless skin covered in microscopic taste buds. Next is its ear, part of its swim bladder no less, and finally, those whiskerish barbs that protrude from its hideous head. The catfish, however, isn't out to win Mississippi Basin beauty contests. When properly filleted and cooked, this freshwater, almost boneless fish can make for a succulent supper. Its flaky flesh has overtones of the muddy waters this fish likes to swim in, but that simply adds to the catfish culture of this Southern specialty. Enjoy it with banjo music in the background.

Trivia Tidbit

Along with the freshwater eel, catfish is a forbidden food in Judaism.

Crappit Heids

If you like fish heads, then crappit heids (also called crappit heads) is the dish for you. This Scottish delicacy is made by stuffing oatmeal, suet and onions into haddock or codfish heads and boiling them to oblivion. Occasionally, fish intestines are shoved into those gruesome, fishy heads, too. Crappit heids aren't as commonplace as they used to be. Other oddly named Scots dishes only the bravest dare to try include clootie dumplin' (a dessert pudding), fife bannocks (flat wheat cakes baked on a griddle), howtowdie (chicken stuffed with oats), cabbie claw (cod with egg sauce and horseradish) or the eyebrow-raising fitless cock (oatmeal pudding molded into the shape of a chicken).

Haggamuggie

In Celtic cooking, muggies are fish stomachs. Can you guess what a haggamuggie is? Think of a haggis made from an oversized, smelly fish. The haggamuggie (also called hugga or hakka muggie) is a Shetland Island dish consisting of the stomach, or muggie, of a big fish stuffed with oatmeal and chopped fish. To make it, wash the stomach, tie one end with string, season a cod liver with salt and pepper, slice it up, stuff it in the stomach along with the oatmeal (but not too full, as the oatmeal will expand), tie the other end and boil it in salted water for 30 minutes. Serve with bread, then try and pronounce haggamuggie with your full mouth.

Imitation Seafood

Is it real, or is it fake? You might use that phrase when it comes to furs or diamonds, but what about fish? Imitation seafood, whether it's crab, scallop or lobster, is actually minced whitefish and, surprise, it isn't a newfangled idea. The process of turning fish meat into elaborate seafood dates back 1000 years to when the Japanese discovered that heating fish caused it to gel, allowing it to be formed into a type of fish cake. Today, a dash of flavoring is added and, presto, "crab" for half the price.

Shark Fin Soup

Don't bother trying to order shark fin soup in restaurants such as Hong Kong Disneyland or European Parliament cafeterias. This luxury soup is now banned from these and other eco-conscious eateries around the world. Although demand for shark fin has increased as many Asians grow more affluent, conservationists point to the declining shark population and the horrific method used to collect fins. Fetching at least $40 each, the fins are often cut off live sharks. Since the rest of the flesh is less valuable, their dying bodies are subsequently thrown back into the sea like garbage. Millions of sharks are killed each year, just for their fins. While the fin is rather tasteless, it separates into long, thin, chewy strands of cartilage that give this expensive soup its renowned gelatinous consistency.

Shark Meat

They've been swimming the seas for hundreds of million of years, but sharks have met their match when it comes to people. When the occasional human becomes a shark's dinner, headlines tout Jaws as the demon of the deep, but shark attacks are rare. Far more shark turns up in people's mouths than vice versa. Shark cartilage is also marketed as an unproven cancer cure despite the fact that sharks themselves can get cancer. When cooked, shark meat turns firm and white and is served as shark teriyaki, shark steaks and shark sandwiches. One caveat, besides possible high mercury levels, is the fact that urea in shark blood breaks down after the fish dies and can make shark meat poisonous, or at the very least smell like pee.

Hákarl

Most of us won't eat rotten fish. Except the Icelanders. They go so far as to make putrefied shark meat, or *hákarl*, a national custom. Traditionally served during the midwinter festival, hákarl may date back to Viking days. To make this Nordic delicacy, first bury a gutted side of shark in gravel for six to eight weeks (the more modern way is to soak it in brine), then allow it to cool in a shack for a couple of months. After it's cured, cut off the thick, brown crust on the skin (since sharks pee through their skin, some say this crust smells like solid urine chunks) to reveal the edible white flesh. Supposedly, hákarl has the same flavor profile as moldy cheese soaked in nuclear waste, which may explain why it is often followed with a shot of *brennivin*, an alcoholic drink made from potatoes.

Sea Cucumber

The sea cucumber (also known as the *trepang* or *bêche-de-mer*) sounds far more tasty than its other name, the sea slug, but this bottom-feeder is no veggie. Sea cucumbers are related to sea stars and sea urchins, except they are phallus-shaped. Some species are even covered in warty bumps. If that isn't enough, the sea cucumber breathes through its anus and spits out sticky threads of white slime (actually its intestines) from the other end when scared or squeezed. So why would any-one want to eat an overgrown slug? Sea cucumbers aren't exactly fast food of the sea. First, there's the trepanging, or sea cucumber harvest. Once collected, they must be gutted, soaked and boiled, then soaked again and dried before cooking. They tend to take on the flavor of whatever broth or sauce they're thrown into, but a sliced, squishy sea cucumber has its admirers. With its looks, that's a good thing.

TENTACLE DELIGHTS

Octopus

Cephalopod aficionados throughout Asia and the Mediterranean often eat octopus steamed or grilled with a zesty side sauce. They come in all sizes, from tiny, fork-sized babies to larger, tougher ones, though many westerners are a little slow to embrace these eight-armed creatures. Maybe it is the fact that the octopus shoots out ink, or that its gelatinous skin changes color to escape predators.

Then again, those rubbery tentacles and chewy suction cups aren't exactly appetizing appendages for many of us. Most frozen octopus is already cleaned, so there's no need to scoop out gross innards. Slow simmering keeps the octopus flesh tender for warm dishes, but its fishy flavor turns up in other foods, such as octopus chips.

Squid and Cuttlefish

Get more bang for your buck with squid or cuttlefish. These super-fast sea creatures swim by jet propulsion and have eight arms plus two extra tentacles, compared to the octopus, which only has eight. As for texture, squid and cuttlefish only taste rubbery and chewy when over-cooked. Even frozen, squid keeps its tender flavor, and while cuttlefish is usually imported to North America from Europe (and more expensive), both should be white and firm when sold fresh and cleaned at the fishmonger. Whatever you do, don't eat the little knife-like beak—it's super sharp. What to do with the ink, the liquid squirted from their sacs for protection? Cook those rubbery cephalopods in it, of course. Mixed with white wine and butter, the ink makes an accompanying "black sauce" for added seafood flavor. In Japan, raw, thinly sliced squid is paired with a fermented fish sauce, and stuffed squid is a favorite in many countries. But most of us know deep-fried squid by its more appetizing name, calamari.

Cod Tongues

Thank cod for cod tongues. Like chicken wings, the tongues of Atlantic cod were once throwaway parts, but they eventually became a familiar food, on the Atlantic Coast, at least. At just under $10 a pound, six or eight battered bits of flesh from a fish's throat can be ordered in many Newfoundland restaurants. They're often topped with scrunchions, crispy, salted pork bits. Eat them just for the halibut. Ha ha!

Lutefisk

Ah, Norway—land of cross-country skiing, trolls and lute-fisk. What is lutefisk, you ask? First debone, gut and skin a codfish. Then salt it and hang it to dry for weeks until it resembles a mummified fishy alien. The stink will be atrocious, but take the cod remnants down and soak them in lye (that caustic stuff made from wood ashes). Don't immerse the fish for too long, or you'll have soap that smells like the back alley of a seafood market after a long weekend. The resulting jelly blob that resembles something a zombie puked up is lutefisk.

Surströmming

If you hold your nose around opened tins of moist cat food, don't ever go near a can of *surströmming*. The fish chunks floating in brown liquid that make up this Swedish delicacy smell so rotten that even pampered housecats may refuse a bite. Swedes who love their national dish insist surströmming is merely soured herring preserved in a tin. After months of "maturing" in barrels, the herring is canned, but the gas-producing fermentation process continues, often causing the cans to bulge slightly. Major airlines have called the tins "potentially explosive" and banned them from flights, although it's more likely they were afraid an inadvertently punctured can could send an unforgettable stink bomb throughout the plane.

HOW 'BOUT THEM CLAMS?

Geoduck Clam

These West Coast burrowing bivalves grow huge—so huge that some of the older ones likely weigh more than your housecat. They also dig deep into the sand, and collecting, make that yanking, them for clambakes or seafood restaurant fare is no easy task. The geoduck clams—use the slang term, gooey duck—have long, thick necks that ooze out saltwater like a leaky faucet. Make no mistake, these are succulent mollusks with a sweet, scallop-like meat that fetches high prices in overseas (and often illegal) markets.

Quahog Clams

Also called the cherrystone or littleneck clam, the American quahog clam is smaller and tastier when compared to its larger cousin, the ocean quahog clam. Usually found in Atlantic waters, the hard, colorful shells of quahog clams were made into beads by coastal Native tribes. In 2007, scientists discovered the world's oldest living animal off the coast of Iceland—a quahog clam that they nicknamed Ming, after the Chinese dynasty when it was born. Believed to be over 405 years old, the unfortunate clam met its demise when researchers had to cut through its shell to count the growth rings. No word on whether the rest of Ming ended up as clam chowder.

Gooseneck Barnacles

From a distance, colonies of mottled gooseneck barnacles vaguely resemble young geese, their whitish tips glistening in the sun like little birdy beaks. Hundreds of years ago, in the days before migration was understood, people thought a certain species of wintering goose developed from this crustacean. Since "barnacle geese," as the birds were nicknamed, came from seafood, they were guiltlessly consumed on Fridays and during Lent, when meat was a religious no-no. The hermaphrodite gooseneck barnacle, also known as the *percebe* in Spanish, has a mussel-like flavor, but this delicacy can be hard to harvest. The edible foot practically cements itself to rocky coastlines, requiring a certain daring expertise just to pry them off. Eat these barnacles boiled with laurel leaves, then remove the leathery skin just above the tip and enjoy the sweet, fruity taste.

Conch Cuisine

If escargots symbolize romance and refinement, then conch represents a wild romp on a beach. Both conches and snails belong to the mollusk family—call them edible cousins. Colonists who migrated to Key West from the Bahamas were also given the name "conch," partly because their diet included this oversized sea snail, and also because many of them stated they would rather eat conch than fight in the American Revolution. They had a point. While conch is now illegal to harvest in U.S. waters and most now come from the Caribbean, the tasty meat doesn't have fishy overtones and reminds one of scallop. Fresh conch is best tenderized and cut up into bite-sized pieces for conch cuisine such as chowder, salad or deep-fried conch fritters. In the Bahamas, conch sometimes goes by its other name, "hurricane ham."

Abalone

Remember those pretty, iridescent shells on jewelry and fashionable hair combs? The meat of abalone is every bit as exquisite. Abalone farms ensure a steady supply of these mollusks for their enthusiasts. Preparing abalone can be messy, hard work. Cut up the flesh, but try not to open the gut, or half-digested kelp will spill out all over your kitchen counter. Pound the meat to tenderize it, then lightly batter and fry it. Clean up the leftover shell and display it as a conversation piece.

CHAPTER 8

Bug-Delicious

HOP TO IT

Come on over to the bug side and join the international majority. To over two-thirds of humanity, insects are an essential commodity, a survival food and frequently a flavorsome snack. Essentially, they're good eats. Some may think of these creepy crawlies as ugly or dirty pests, but there are many reasons to indulge in a bite of bug. For one they're nutritious, low in cholesterol and high in amino acids, essentially fatty acids and protein (often 30 to 70 percent of their body weight). They're also plentiful. Insects comprise over 90 percent of all the animals on this planet. You literally can't go anywhere without stepping on one. Historically, this overabundance of "microlivestock," or "microfauna," as it's been dubbed, has spawned a growth in crawler cuisine.

For many countries, the insect taboo doesn't exist. In India, green weaver ant paste is used as a condiment for curry. Sago worms are a specialty in Papua New Guinea, and the Thais enjoy termite treats or weaver ants and eggs mixed with sticky rice. Mexicans, too, have a tradition of turning insects into delectable delicacies. Big-city restaurants even cater to upscale clientele seeking such pre-Hispanic dishes as *gusanos*, or deep-fried maguey worms. At many crowded Southeast Asian markets, the variety of available insects is so overwhelming that potential buyers practically require an entomology degree. Where there's demand, there's a profit to be made. Villagers often supplement their rice farming income, and fill up their own larders, by trapping insects at night. Baited with a blue-violet fluorescent light, the insects, including crickets, water bugs and others, fall into bowls of water, where they are collected the following morning. Seasoned, ready-to-eat insects are even canned and exported to global markets. Slowly, the "bugs as food" campaign is taking hold in developed nations. Specialty markets and Internet and novelty stores now stock such exotic nibbles as scorpion lollipops, salt 'n' vinegar dried crickets and seasoned larvae snacks. Perhaps we could all use insect-inspired cooking lessons to enhance our critter culinary skills. Well-prepared bugs shouldn't give would-be insect eaters butterflies in the stomach. Microwaved moth, anyone?

Grasshopper and Locusts

Of all the edible insects, sugary-sweet grasshoppers are perhaps the most prevalent. An indispensable food for indigenous peoples worldwide, Native Americans ate them, too, and often baked them into a type of fruitcake. In Africa, ground grasshoppers make a hummus-like paste, while in Mexico, heaps of these little leapers are collected in large clay pots, boiled, seasoned and dried into tangy chapulines. In Thailand, they're squished until the insides pop out and munched raw or fried in oil. Locust, the grasshopper's swarm-loving cousin, can be prepared in a similar fashion. The Old Testament mentions plagues of locusts but permits them as food. Even John the Baptist survived on locusts in the desert. Because they like to fly, it's recommended to pick off the wings, head and legs first. Gut them, then barbecue them on a stick or fry them in a wok for a "crispy on the outside, creamy sweet on the inside" snack.

Grasshopper Tortilla Recipe

Collect about 1000 grasshoppers (the smaller, the better).

Soak in water for one day.

Boil the bugs and let them dry.

Sauté onion, garlic, a small amount of lemon or lime juice and salt in a pan.

Add grasshoppers and gently stir-fry for a few minutes.

Wrap the mixture in flour tortillas along with chili sauce and guacamole. Enjoy.

Did You Know?

The great 19th-century French artist, Henri de Toulouse-Lautrec, was also a creative cook who enjoyed grilled grasshoppers seasoned with salt and pepper.

CRUNCH and MUNCH

Beetles

It's a bug's life out there, but in many countries, if you're a beetle, your days may be numbered. While beetle larvae make a juicier treat, the hard-shelled adults are nothing to grumble about. For instance, in Thailand, giant water beetles are eaten whole, ground into a paste or stir-fried with mushrooms, onions, chili and garlic. In parts of Mexico, toasted beetles turn up in a various dishes. Raw jumilies, a member of the stinkbug family, apparently taste like salted sesame seeds but smell like cinnamon when crushed and are used to add oomph to salsa sauces. These little stinkers have a reputation for living up to a week after being beheaded. Try them in a lively salsa or dip for your next Super Bowl party.

Fly Delicacy

Even in cold northern climates, flies buzz around looking for something to eat and often end up being eaten. One type of botfly, the warble, seeks out large, warm animals and lays its eggs on the skin or in the noses of caribou. When the eggs hatch, the larvae burrow into the animal's skin for the winter, creating swollen bumps along the caribous' backs. These bumps fill with liquid and can be squeezed until the fly larvae pop out like candy from a gooey Pez dispenser. Samuel Hearne, the 18th-century northern explorer, described some of these protein-rich larvae, which the Arctic peoples ate alive, as being quite large and "said by those who liked them as fine as gooseberries." Although Hearne wrote that he ate caribou stomach, he drew the line at "lice and warbles."

Cicadas

Aristotle pondered deep-fried thoughts while he snacked on cicadas. The ancient philosopher wrote of the tasty nymphs and prized "females full of white eggs." Evidently, these harmless bugs taste good and are good for you. Since cicadas are vegetarian insects, you won't find any pre-digested bug parts in their crunchy bodies. They've been an important food of Aboriginal cultures around the world, including North America. Every 17 years, like clockwork, swarms of cicadas emerge to buzz the northeastern U.S. The event draws media attention and a flurry of cicada recipes. Foodie thrill seekers gobble roasted cicadas down like peanuts or use them as a crispy pizza topping.

Crickets

It's a no-brainer. A farmer uses 100 pounds of grain to produce 16 pounds of steak, but the same amount of grain produces 50 pounds of crickets. Approximately 180 crickets have the same number of calories as two slices of bread. Widely munched in Asia, more westerners should discover that they, too, can enjoy crunchy crickets, if only for ecological and nutritional reasons. Crickets pack huge amounts of protein in their tiny bodies and make excellent toppers for stuffed tomatoes or fancy hors d'oeuvres. Consumers can even purchase them in bulk (they're as close as your neighborhood pet store). So why the reluctance to consume crickets? Perhaps they remind us of a certain Jiminy who sang about wishing on a star for his long-nosed friend.

Cricket Cookies

2 1/4 cups flour
1 tsp baking soda
1 tsp salt
1 cup butter, softened
3/4 cup sugar
3/4 cup brown sugar
1 tsp vanilla
2 eggs
1 12-ounce package of chocolate chips
1 cup chopped nuts
1/2 cup dry-roasted crickets

Preheat oven to 375°F. In a small bowl, combine flour, baking soda and salt, and set aside. In a large bowl, combine butter, sugar, brown sugar and vanilla, and beat until creamy. Beat in eggs. Gradually add the flour mixture and insects, and mix well. Stir in chocolate chips. Drop by rounded teaspoonfuls onto an ungreased cookie sheet. Bake for 8 to 10 minutes.

(Reprinted with permission from WildRecipes.com.)

Cockroaches

Never underestimate the lowly cockroach. These creepy-crawlies have endured 300 million years on this earth and could likely outlive most species in the event of a nuclear war or other planetary catastrophe. In 2001, however, a few dozen met their match when a British man won a world record by shoving 36 Madagascar cockroaches down his throat in one minute (they apparently taste like shrimp). While some entomology experts warn that raw cockroaches may harbor parasites, millions catch them in bowls of water overnight, then boil, spice and deep-fry them for a crispy treat. *Olé* to *el cucaracha*.

FLY, BE FREE

Cordyceps

Also known as the vegetable or mushroom caterpillar and in China as the "summer grass, winter worm," cordyceps is one those rare, expensive and often indescribable ingredients. But is it a vegetable or an edible insect? Actually, it is a parasitic fungus (*Cordyceps sinenis*) that infects a hibernating caterpillar and subsequently morphs it into what looks like a cross between a leaf, a caterpillar and a mushroom. Harvested before it produces spores, dried cordyceps has been used for centuries in traditional medicines. On occasion, it appears on menus as part of an elaborate poultry stuffing or floating in a bowl of tonic soup, looking like the mushroomy mummified caterpillar that it actually is.

Bogong Moths

More than a few Australians have taken a page from native Aboriginal menus for coping with the swarms of bogong moths that descend on buildings and windowsills, and clog air-conditioning ducts—they've turned these pests into bite-sized tucker. Moths are high in protein and fat, so they make an ideal high-energy snack. Pull off the wings and flame them to get rid of their natural furriness, then roast them in oil. What does a bogong moth taste like? "Buttered hazelnut," explained one fly-by-night convert.

Dragonflies

Indonesians call them "sky shrimp," but you needn't travel halfway around the world to try dragonflies. An insectarium in the U.S. has become the latest place for budding bug food adventurers. Visitors can learn all about bugs, then buy them for lunch at the cafeteria. The menu includes dragonflies dipped by their wings into a seasoned egg mixture and then quickly fried with sautéed mushrooms. Daring diners at the bug cafeteria say they taste remarkably like crab meat. Now that's weird.

Wasps

Yes, those pesky yellow jackets do have a purpose— they're an awesome protein source. In fact, wasps contain over 81 percent protein, one of the highest. Emperor Hirohito of Japan enjoyed fried wasps mixed with rice and soy sauce. Mexicans also eat wasps, and the larvae are relished in rural Southeast Asian countries such as

Thailand and Laos. Enjoy them quickly stir-fried and aggressively seasoned, especially if you think they deserve it.

Baby Bee Larvae

Is it any surprise to learn that bees taste sweet? (They do make honey, after all.) Various cultures from the Congolese to the Chinese, Laotians and Native Americans consume bees, most often in the form of "bee brood," or bee larvae. When baked or fried, the result is a flaky, crispy rice-like food with a nutty taste. Gourmet stores in Mexico also sell canned bees in syrup or coated in chocolate, and the Nepalese like a bee larvae liquor called *bakuti*, which is made from giant honeybee brood.

Waiter, I'd Like a Fly in My Soup

Don't think you'll ever eat a bug? Think again. The average North American eats over one pound of insects per year. Yes, we are all guilty of entomaphagy, or eating insects. Believe it or not, government food safety regulations permit some microscopic bug bits, even rodent filth, euphemistically termed "natural contaminants," in food processing. For example, the FDA allows up to 35 fruit fly eggs per cup of raisins, one or more rodent hairs per 50 grams (almost 2 ounces) of wheat flour and one or more maggots per cup of canned citrus fruit juice. And 100 grams (3.5 ounces) of peanut butter can contain up to 30 or more insect parts. The average chocolate bar may include three to five insect legs, and salads likely have more, but it's usually hard to find them through all that ranch dressing.

NOT SO ITSY-BITSY SPIDERS and SCORPIONS

Tarantulas

Tasty tarantulas are definitely not for arachnophobes— or maybe they are? What better way to overcome a fear of spiders than to chow down on one, two or three? In Cambodia, consuming arachnids became common when villagers were faced with starvation during the Khmer Rouge years. Today street vendors serve *a-ping*, or spiders fried in garlic, for about a dime apiece. Not a bad deal when you consider that's eight crunchy legs to pull off and a juicy, white-meat body to devour (but watch out for the brownish gunk in the abdomen). The spiders, which are actually a type of tarantula, are bred for market or found in forests. No worries, as their poisonous fangs are removed before cooking. Make sure the hairy legs have been burned smooth, since finding a hair in your mouth can ruin the fun. Alternately, try spider wine, a traditional Asian tonic made from fermented rice with a spider floating in it.

GRILLED SPIDERS

BUG-DELICIOUS

Scorpions

When you're stranded in the desert (or forest, cave, wherever) look no further than the scorpion for a succulent survival food. Hunt these critters at night, when they crawl out of their holes and hopefully into the waiting container you strategically placed on the ground. First, stab the scorpion with a thin stick to immobilize it. Next, remove the stinger, which contains venom, then cook the scorpion over an open fire. Scorpion, apparently, ranges from tasting like raw shrimp to popcorn, and they're available fried and skewered in many Asian countries. For those who like ready-to-eat meals, scorpions are also available canned.

> We can eat anything with four legs, except the table. Anything that walks, swims, crawls or flies with its back to heaven is edible.
>
> – Popular Asian saying

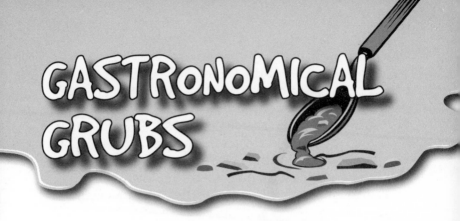

GASTRONOMICAL GRUBS

Silkworms

Silk shirts, scarves and ties all started life as silkworm cocoons. These baby mulberry moths have been harvested for over 5000 years in China for the long, thread-like fibers of their chrysalides. Inside each outer shell is a soft, succulent yellow larva, or worm—the most edible part—that apparently tastes a bit like a soggy, buttered corn kernel. In Korea, they are called *beondegi* and are eaten as a canned snack, like peanuts. They are also canned for export. Silkworm grubs can be cooked in almost any way imaginable—boiled, fried, even ground into a powder and mixed into soups. Buy these tantalizing tidbits steaming hot from street vendors or order a plateful at an Asian restaurant, where they arrive with an accompanying sesame dip. Bet you can't eat just one.

Mopane Worms

They're slow, fat and wriggle through life by munching on the leaves of the mopane tree, but don't be too quick to call mopane worms "lowlifes." They're a million-dollar business in southern Africa and provide much-needed income for locals. Harvesters pull these worms, which can grow up to six inches long, off the leaves by hand. Once picked, mopane worms are pinched to push out their innards, then dried in the sun or smoked. They can be eaten raw (avoid the head, though) or boiled in salt water and fried, but they are also canned in brine and served with tomato sauce. Dried ones can be rehydrated in water. Like silkworms, mopane worm silk is used for garments. Their meat has three times more protein than beef and a mild taste (although some say the dried ones have a woody flavor). In some areas, the mopane population has dwindled because of the harvest. If they aren't plucked for people food, mopane worms eventually turn into adult Emperor moths, which live only a few days.

Earthworms

Remember the kid at school who did anything on a dare, like eating earthworms? As it turns out, he may have been onto something. Sure, they look like thick, wet noodles, but earthworms are not just for the birds. Aboriginal and ancient peoples knew this and made worms part of their diet. Earthworms have no bones and no fat, only a natural earthy flavor. They can't even be called insects because they don't have legs. The wrigglers are easy to find—just dig into the soil in your backyard garden or stop at the local bait shop. Wait until it rains, and they'll come out in droves onto a paved driveway. To prepare earthworms, contain them for a day or two until they expel their waste (if they've been kept in peat moss, no purging is necessary). Wash and dry the earthworms a few times to remove their mucus coating. Place them on a cookie sheet and bake them in an oven for several minutes. Alternately, clean earthworms can be fried in oil or mixed into muffins and meatloaf, but one of the best ways to enjoy them is as a crispy baked snack with a pinch of salt.

Banana Worm Bread

1/2 cup shortening
3/4 cup sugar
2 bananas, mashed
2 cups flour
1 tsp soda
1 tsp salt
1/2 cup chopped nuts
2 eggs
1/4 cup dry-roasted armyworms

Mix together all ingredients. Bake in greased loaf pan at 350°F for about one hour.

(Reprinted with permission from WildRecipes.com.)

Witchetty Grubs

When Prince Charles turned down a chance to eat a live witchetty grub while on a visit to Alice Springs, Australia, in 2005, he passed on a perfect high-protein snack. He could have swallowed this beetle larva in the usual headfirst manner (so the tail stops wiggling) and enjoyed its almond-like flavor. They also taste great barbecued over a wood fire or roasted on hot charcoals. The Aborigines first dug up these white grubs with the black and yellow heads from the roots of the acacia, or witchetty, bush. Today they're sampled by outback tourists and are almost always roasted or stir-fried instead of being eaten squiggly raw.

Huhu Grubs

Australia may have their witchetty grubs, but New Zealand has its *huhu*. The white larvae of this dark-brown native New Zealand beetle, the juicy, fat huhu grubs are found inside dead trees. These protein pick-me-ups have a peanut-butter-like taste and are a traditional Maori delicacy that can be eaten raw, roasted or deep-fried. As an adult beetle, this bug is also known as the "haircutter" because its long antennae and legs can get trapped in hair and must be cut out.

Mosquitoes

These blood-sucking bugs may be the bane of outdoor fun, but there's one way to bite back at them—eat their eggs. Yes, other species besides goldfish find the almost microscopic mosquito eggs a delicacy. In Mexico, a type of water mosquito known as the *axayacatl* lays eggs that produce white larvae called *ahuautili*. Harvested from ponds and lakes, bunches of these ahuautili can be toasted and stuffed into tortillas with a chili sauce. Now that's sweet, and spicy, revenge.

ANTS ON YOUR PLATE

Honeypot Ants

If Winnie the Pooh lived in Australia, he would have loved the honeypot ant. These little insects store plant nectar in their rear ends, though it tastes more like molasses than honey. Bite the ant in the butt and suck the nectar out, just like the juicy center of a squirt-chew candy. Eat the rest of the ant for added thiamine and riboflavin and to stave off those rumblies in your tumbly.

Escamoles

Escamoles are better known by their other name, "Mexican caviar." Sounds appetizing, doesn't it—until you find out they are also called "ant-egg caviar." Relax, they aren't ant eggs. Escamoles are actually ant larvae. Doesn't that go down better? Ant larvae have been a delicacy for centuries, and even the ancient Greeks and Romans enjoyed their nutty flavor. Found in the roots of the agave (or maguey) cactus, the larvae of the large, black *Limetopum* ant, are usually collected during springtime, though some restaurants freeze them for year-round menus. Escamoles taste best fried in butter, then mixed with guacamole or salsa until they look like a dark, soggy cereal. Stuffed in a tortilla or served as a dip, escamoles make a traditional Mexican treat. *Mucho gusto!*

Chocolate-Covered Ants

Let's face it. Chocolate makes anything taste great. Specialty stores and Internet sites sell oodles of confectionery-coated creepy-crawlies. Drizzle dark, milk or white chocolate over tons of tiny ants, and anyone can become a human anteater without the unattractive snout. It may be hard to truly taste those ants in all that candy, but the experience isn't much different than chowing down on chocolate-covered crispy rice. Plus, they include a bonus dose of protein. To whip up your own batch of chocolate-covered ants, you'll need a few tablespoons of ants, preferably fresh from an anthill. Stay away from red ants, as they're too peppery for the sweet chocolate. Mix the ants in with egg yolk, then fold into melted chocolate. Refrigerate until solid. These make great scary Halloween party fare, especially when guests find out what's in the chocolate.

Big Butt Ants

Move over pork rinds and buttered popcorn, the big butt ant queens are coming to town. During the rainy season in the Santander region of Columbia, eager townsfolk harvest virgin, mate-seeking ants with behinds the size of peas. These big butt, fat ass ants, or *hormiga culona* (incidentally, *culona* is also Spanish slang for a lady with an ample derriere), are a species of leafcutter ant known for their micro-power-tool mandibles. At $11 per pound, the locals sell as many of the edible queens as they can catch. They're thought to be beneficial in fighting cancer, curing infertility or as an aphrodisiac, which is why they often turn up as wedding feast snacks. Big butt ants have been roasted and toasted for centuries. One could say these protein-rich booster snacks kick serious butt.

Lemon Ant

Tiny, brown, hardworking—does this sound like a candy treat to you? Pop one in your mouth, and its tangy juices tingle your taste buds like a lemon drop. Lemon ant colonies, some of which are hundreds of years old, live on trees (the lemon ant tree) that all the other rainforest trees avoid. Besides having a citrus flavor, the ants produce their own herbicide, a type of formic acid, which inhibits other trees from growing nearby. Stumble across one, and you've stepped into the legendary devil's garden, a puzzling clearing in the middle of the jungle, except for one lemon ant tree. Lemon ants are also taken to soothe sore throats and help cure the flu, but most people outside the jungle settle for a lozenge instead.

Did You Know?

Toasted termites are eaten in many countries, and the queen termite is considered a delicacy in Thai bug cuisine.

Pest Control

In late July 2008, a 52-year-old Australian exterminator took his flashlight, a pocketknife and a metal detector, and then went out prospecting in the rocky desert outback. When he failed to return to camp, his fellow prospectors called police. Four days later, local Aborigines found him, dehydrated but alive. He had survived by eating termites for moisture and protein. "Termites don't taste too bad," he later admitted at a news conference.

CHAPTER 9

Crazy Cuisine Olympics

NAME THAT FOOD

Have you ever ordered off a menu only to be served a dish that bears no resemblance to what it's called? Welcome to the wonderful world of weird food names. The list began sometime around the dawn of language and hasn't stopped since. Below is merely a sampling of the countless culinary experiments that have survived to modern times. Almost all unusual food descriptions are steeped in cultural significance. It's not hard to figure out where some dishes get their names, but others can confuse even the most learned linguist. Of course, when that hunk of uncooked hamburger with an egg on top arrives in front of you (and you thought you asked for a steak with tartar sauce on the side), will you eat it? Perhaps we could all broaden our culinary horizons with a little unexpected food exploration. Try it. You might like it.

Bangers and Mash

This classic working-class, meat-and-potatoes meal consists of English sausages and mashed potatoes soaked with an onion gravy. Heating the sausages can cause the membrane-thin casing to burst and make a sharp "bang" sound, hence the name "bangers." The mash is what happens when boiled potatoes are pulverized.

> If you ate pasta and antipasto, would you still be hungry?
>
> – Unknown

Beavertail

Bet you didn't know there are two kinds of beavertail. The first, naturally, is the actual tail of this orthodontically challenged rodent. Early colonists were permitted to eat beaver on Fridays (since beavers swim in water, the Pope classified them as "fishy"). Not wanting to waste a single appendage, settlers cut off the beaver's paddle-like tail, held it over a fire until the skin fell off and threw the remaining meaty part into a stew with beans.

The other kind of beavertail is a flat, narrow loaf that dates back to the 19th century. Back then, a blob of dough was stretched into a shape resembling a beaver's tail and carefully held by sticks over an open fire pit until it was cooked. Today, deep-fried beavertails (and similar treats called elephant ears) are topped with a sprinkling of sugar and cinnamon and sold from kiosks at fall fairs and yuppie outdoor markets.

Bubble and Squeak

Bubble and squeak may sound like cartoon characters, a clown duo or twin hamsters but, surprise, it's mashed potato served with shredded cabbage and onions fried in butter. A slice of corned beef—a spiced canned meat, Spam's rival—often accompanies this traditional British cuisine.

Caesar Salad

Et tu, salad? This well-known salad was not named after the ancient Roman Julius Caesar. In fact, the famous Roman probably never ate one in his life. Cesare Cardini, an Italian Mexican, takes the credit for tossing up the greens in a Tijuana restaurant back in 1924. The mixture included romaine lettuce and croutons with a garlicky vinaigrette dressing of olive oil, egg, black pepper, lemon juice and a sprinkle of Parmesan cheese. Sorry fish lovers, anchovies were not an original ingredient.

Carpetbag Steak

This conjures up images of slabs of raw meat shoved into an old fabric suitcase. Carpetbag steak is actually a rare, broiled filet mignon stuffed with oysters. One would think they would invent a more gourmet handle for such a classy dish.

Chicken of the Sea

On her reality television show, Jessica Simpson said she thought Chicken of the Sea contained chicken. Wrong. Poor Jessica had fallen for the marketing campaign of a seafood company that became the first to can light tuna. Its product became so successful that the company even renamed itself Chicken of the Sea and now sells salmon and shrimp products as well as tuna.

Cock-a-Leekie

This unusually named soupy Scottish stew contains chicken broth (that's where the cock comes from), leeks (that's where the leekie term comes from), barley, thyme and, traditionally (of all things), stewed prunes. The prunes give the dish a distinctive flavor, but they may be omitted or served separately for those wishing to avoid any form of laxative. Traditionally, this soup was made from the loser of a cockfight and accompanies haggis. Slurp it down while watching *Braveheart*.

Dirty Rice

Dirty rice isn't a bowl of rice that fell on the floor only to be scooped back in and immediately served (the five-second rule, right?). It's a Caribbean and Cajun specialty consisting of plain rice cooked with chicken giblets and seasonings. Almost anything can be thrown into the rice (except dirt), and while it may not have that pristine white appearance, dirty rice makes for an aromatic, appetizing meal, despite its name.

French Fries

Like the Statue of Liberty, French fries are a symbol of America—imported from France. These strips of deep-fried potato likely originated in France and Belgium, when street vendors sold them as *frites*. Their popularity grew throughout the 19th century, and even Charles Dickens wrote about French fries in *A Tale of Two Cities*, describing them as "husky chips of potatoes fried with some reluctant drops of oil." French fries finally immigrated to North America during the 1880s, and the rest, as they say, is history.

Fufu

If you fancied play dough as a child, you'll flip over *fufu*. Not only is its name kid-friendly (alternate spellings of *foo foo* or *foufou* are equally charming), but this African staple is meant to be eaten with (clean) bare hands. No forks, spoons or utensils necessary. Fufu variations appear all over the continent, even across the ocean in Caribbean countries (there is also a Hawaiian version called *poi* made from mashed taro root). Most fufu-type foods are derived from vegetables such as yams, cassavas, plantains or rice. These starches undergo an intense, lengthy pounding with a large, wooden stick, then they're boiled and pounded again until they become a glutinous, sticky mass comparable to wet cookie dough. Fufu sits in a bowl of soup or stew until you pluck out a small chunk. Roll it into a ball, stick your thumb in it and you've got a handy fufu-holder for the rest of the mixture. When the soup or stew is gone, eat the fufu-holder. Fast fufu is also available in an instant, just-add-water powder, no pounding required. It's attractive to bachelors, harried housewives and, now, African ex-pats who can find this ethnic processed food in specialty stores throughout the U.S. and Canada.

Glass Noodles

Ingesting glass of any kind is definitely not recommended, nor is it nutritious, but don't hesitate to try delicious glass noodles. Made from green mung bean paste (mung is such a mouth-watering word, isn't it?), these wiry, thin, cellophane-like noodles are often used in Asian cooking. Also called bean thread noodles, Chinese vermicelli or *woon-sen* in Thai, they're gluten-free and a healthier alternative to regular wheat noodles. Once boiled, glass noodles quickly turn transparent so you can see right through them.

Trivia Tidbit

Noodles are a symbol of longevity and have been eaten in Asia since 200 BC.

Grape-Nuts

In 1897, Charles Post marketed his Grape-Nuts, a breakfast cereal made of whole-grain wheat flour, malted barley flour, salt and yeast. Oddly enough, there were no grapes or nuts in the cereal. But why call it Grape-Nuts and not Healthy Cereal or something more appropriate? One reason was that the cereal contained grape sugar, but another explanation was that it resembled grape seeds or little nuts. Either way, the product eventually became a hit among health nuts. As their motto states, Grape-Nuts "fill you up, not out."

Grunt

How do you make a blueberry grunt? Kick it in the berries. Well, not really. Grunt, also known as betty, slump, buckle, crisp, crumble, cobbler and (when flipped upside down) sonker, is basically a doughy dessert filled with fruit and often covered in a crumbly topping. Grunts and their kin date back to colonial times, when settlers attempted to recreate the classic British steamed pudding. The grunt was apparently named after the "grunting" noise the fruit made as it cooked.

Hangtown Fry

An omelet of eggs, oysters and bacon—does that sound like the last meal for a convict about to be hanged? The name Hangtown fry may also have been coined after a California town frequented by miners during the Gold Rush. The successful ones were rumored to order the priciest meal available, the local "fry."

Hardtack

Question: Where can you find hardtack?

a) Hardware store
b) Equestrian club
c) Liquor store
d) None of the above

The answer is d) because hardtack is another term for ship biscuits, or pilot or sea bread. Developed in the 1800s, this plain cracker or biscuit is tough enough to dull a tooth. The harder, the better, since this makes it more resistant to mold and maggots. Try this Civil War staple at reenactments, if you don't mind gnawing on a brick.

Hominy and Grits

What's this on the breakfast menu—ham, eggs and *grits*?
No worries, since the grits aren't eggshells or bird gravel.
They're made from big or coarse hominy, a dried, hulled
corn. The hominy is then ground to a rough, sandy texture
and called "little hominy" or "grits." This basic southern U.S.
carbohydrate could be the country's first processed food.
Native Americans showed the colonists how to prepare the
corn by soaking it in water and wood ashes until the hulls
fell off. In colonial times, corn was ground in a samp mill—
basically a tree stump and a wooden block—and big hominy
still goes by the name of "samp." Hominy and grits were the
settler's instant cereal, like the English oatmeal porridge
or "hasty pudding." Today, you can buy canned hominy
(no soaking required), but the best grits come from the
carefully milled stuff. In Mexico, big hominy is mixed with
pork, chilies and spices into a satisfying stew called *pozole*.
Ground even finer, the dried corn makes tortilla flour. Grits
and hominy are considered both a cereal and a vegetable, so
chowing down on them during any meal knocks off two food
groups with one item. Used in baked goods, side dishes or
made into a patty and fried, grits are one of those comfort
foods that memories are made of. More grits, please

Hoosh

If you're planning a trip to explore the Antarctic, you'd
better like hoosh. This hearty stew of dried meat (or
pemmican), fat, oats or ship biscuits, and potatoes, when
available, filled the stomachs of explorers such as Ernest
Shackleton and Robert Scott. Plentiful penguins (to quote
from an old Warner Brothers cartoon, "they're pwactically
chickens") were often the meat in hoosh. Today, goose
is a better substitute, especially since penguins aren't
available for consumption, unless you're a seal or other
Antarctic native.

Hotchpotch

Not to be confused with the childhood street game (hopscotch) or a mishmash jumble (hodgepodge), this meat-and-vegetable mixture also goes by the name of hotchpotch, hutspot, hot pot or hochepot. The meat can be oxtail, beef, chicken or pig's ears, feet and tails, while the vegetables are usually cabbage, carrots, onions and potatoes. Throw them together into a pot, cook with stock and, *ta-da*, hotchpotch.

Hush Puppies

The dog might eat your slippers, but you can get him back by eating hush puppies. Fortunately, it's not dog meat, but rather a southern U.S. dish of fried cornmeal balls with onions and seasoning. The name apparently comes from hunters who would try to "hush up" their barking dogs with leftover cornmeal batter.

Junket

The word "junket" is occasionally used to describe a vacation. The other meaning is an ancient sweetened milk dessert, set with rennet and often topped with chocolate flakes or nutmeg. A favorite with kids, and definitely not a junk food, homemade junkets were a standard dessert in Britain and European countries before the packaged ones took over.

Mannish Water

Ya, mon, this potent Jamaican soup includes goat head meat, goat feet, goat tripe, green bananas, yams, spices and a splash of rum. Throw in a goat testicle, and it definitely lives up to its name, mannish water—a pseudo-aphrodisiac referred to as "power water that will make him strong as a bull." Look for mannish water at roadside stands next to the roasted yams, instead of at fancy tourist restaurants.

Mincemeat

Mincemeat is to Christmas what pumpkin pie is to Thanksgiving—traditional holiday baking. So why doesn't mincemeat contain any meat? Traditionally, it did, as well as beef or ox tongue, chicken, eggs, raisins and spices. A 16th-century recipe describes mincemeat as "pyes of mutton or beif...fine minced and seasoned." Today, mincemeat tarts or pies forgo the meaty parts in lieu of chopped dried fruit, brandy and spices mixed with beef suet (or shortening for vegetarians). Often presented as a warm winter dessert, mincemeat, like a fine wine, gets better with age and can be stored for years.

Pâté Chinois

Translated from French as "Chinese pie," *pâté chinois* has nothing to do with China. With its layers of ground beef and corn topped with mashed potatoes, this dish resembles more of an English shepherd's pie or Greek moussaka than anything Asian. Where pâté chinois got its name is debatable, and there's no trace of it in cookbooks prior to the 20th century. Chinese immigrant cooks may have introduced it to French Canadian railway workers during the late 19th century. Similarly, the dish may have been brought back by Quebeckers working in the Maine town of China. Pâté chinois remains a favorite family food, especially when covered in ketchup.

Pig-in-a-Blanket

Remember the scene from *Charlotte's Web* where the little girl, Fern, cradles Wilbur, the piglet, like a baby in   a soft blanket? The other kind of pig-in-a-blanket is more enticing. Essentially, it's a sausage wrapped in bacon (United Kingdom), a hot dog wrapped in cheese and dough (United States) or a wiener wrapped in puff pastry (Germany). In some European countries, the term also refers to a stuffed cabbage roll covered in tomato sauce. Sausages in mashed potatoes are also called "zeppelins in a fog."

Poutine

French Canadian foodies are known for their love of poutine. Pou...what? Think heart attack on a plate, or French fries smothered in hot gravy and melted cheese curds. Artery-clogging poutine is not recommended for anyone watching his or her cholesterol, but this greasy dish is sloppily delicious and perfect for cold, snowy evenings. Order it in southern France, though, and you may be disappointed. There, poutine means fried young sardines or anchovies.

Quark and Quawk

Is quark an astronomical entity or a hypothetical atomic particle in physics? Neither, at least when it comes to snacks. Quark is a yogurt-like, sour-cream pudding often infused with vanilla essence or fruit. Not to be confused with quawk (or quaq), from the Inuit word for "frozen meat," which can be, but is not limited to, ice-cold raw seal, caribou or Arctic fish meat—the original flash-frozen dinner.

Shoofly Pie

It's not hard to guess where shoofly pie got its name. Like a super-sweet coffee cake, this settler original has a molasses and brown sugar filling and a crumbly topping. Add chocolate icing to turn it into chocolate shoofly pie. The bottom is either "dry" or "wet" depending on how much flour is used. No doubt about it, this dessert is so sticky that flies, and hungry kids, are attracted to it.

Spam

Approximately six billion cans of Spam or "spiced ham" have been produced since this wartime canned meat was developed in 1937. Talk about Spam, a lot. If put together, end to end, all those cans would circle the Earth 15 times. This meat in a tin is also Hawaii's official state food.

Spotted Dick

Of all the nicknames for sponge pudding, spotted dick definitely ranks as one of the oddest. While it might raise some eyebrows, the "dick" in this dessert originally meant either "dough" or "sticky." The "spotted" part stands for the raisins or dried fruit. Back in the old days, spotted dick was made with boiled beef suet and bread-crumbs. It's still served as a baked suet pudding and sometimes as a steamed sponge one, each lavishly smothered in hot custard. Recent attempts to change the name spotted dick to the less laughable "spotted Richard" have failed.

Sweetbread

It's neither sweet nor a bread and probably wins the "most-unlike-what-you-thought-it-was" prize. Sweetbread is the culinary term for the thymus gland and pancreas of a cow, pig or lamb. Like brains, sweetbreads should be soaked in cold water first to make the membranes easier to remove (no further surgery required). They can then be blanched and grilled, roasted or braised in wine, stock and vegetables. Calves' sweetbreads make flavorsome fritters, though deep-frying probably turns anything, including glands, into great tasting food.

foodie Fact

Order some *mollejas* in Argentina, and you'll get sweetbreads.

Toad-in-the-Hole

This unusually named dish consists of sausages cooked in Yorkshire pudding batter. Rest assured that no amphibians are used to make toad-in-the-hole.

Tomatoes of a Different Stripe

What's green with yellowish stripes? A zebra tomato, of course. This two-toned tomato makes a great preserve or salad ingredient and, best of all, doesn't squirt in your mouth like its cherry bomb cousin.

If you're into colorful veggies (though tomatoes are technically a fruit, food legalese experts have declared it a vegetable, so there), go for the new purple tomatoes. Thanks to two extra genes from the snapdragon flower, this tomato sports an eggplant hue and extra antioxidants. That said, green tomato lovers have always passed over the classic crimson kind for pale green ones with a firmer, tarter flesh. Fried in bacon drippings or vegetable oil, green tomatoes are the perfect side dish. Once you go green, red is so passé.

Welsh Rarebit

Also called Welsh rabbit, this quick and easy grilled snack is not rare and has nothing to do with rabbits. It's toast topped with cheddar, mustard, pepper, an optional egg yolk, a little splash of pale ale and Worcestershire sauce.

Wow Wow Sauce

The name of this sauce definitely belongs in the unusual names category, even if it was first used in the early 19th century. Wow wow sauce contains bouillon, port wine, mustard, pickled cucumbers, parsley and walnuts. Its inventor, Dr. William Kitchiner, was a telescope maker and a cook who obviously had a thing for exciting condiments.

LET IT ROT

Fermented Fish Sauce

There's something about fermented fish sauce that makes all other condiments pale by comparison. As distasteful as it sounds, rotten fish juice is well liked worldwide, and virtually every culture has its own form of this pungent sauce. Modern fish-based sauces can trace their origins back to garum, an ancient liquid made from macerated fish leftovers. Garum was to the Greeks and Romans what ketchup is to most westerners today. In the 1st century AD, Pliny the Elder wrote of garum "mixed with wine," and the *Apicius* cookbook frequently mentions the sauce. To make garum, layers of fish blood and guts, herbs and salt were left to rot in the sun and then pulverized into a mixture. Allowed to putrefy for exactly 20 days, the result was an oozing liquid that made a surprisingly savory sauce. This pungent processing raised such a stink that garum making was eventually permitted only on the outskirts of cities. Once

Did You Know?

A batch of garum in Pompeii, containing the remains of a Mediterranean fish prevalent in the summer months, helped confirm the exact date of Mt. Vesuvius' eruption as August 24, 79 AD.

poured and sealed well into amphora bottles (remember, this was before Tupperware), the garum wasn't nearly as offensive.

Stinky Tofu

Follow your nose—it will definitely know where stinky tofu can be found. This smelly substance, known as *chou dofu*, is regular tofu with added yeast. Left for a few days, it ferments into a nauseating little vittle that can be deep-fried and served with chili sauces. They say our sense of smell is 95 percent of how a food tastes, but you may wish to plug your nose when trying stinky tofu. An acquired taste, no doubt.

Tempeh

Similar to tofu, tempeh ranks as a familiar Southeast Asian food but is made from the whole fermented soybean rather than only its milk. The soybeans are first soaked to remove their hulls, heated, and then left to ferment until a white mold of microorganisms slowly covers each soybean. In simple terms, tempeh is a protein-rich, moldy tofu that's *mmm, mmm,* good.

Trivia Tidbit

Zymology (zymurgy) is the study of the process of fermentation.

Miso

You've likely heard of miso soup. But do you know where the miso comes from? Miso is a fermented soybean paste made from rice, barley or wheat to which a yeast mold has been added. Known in Japan for centuries, darker misos tend to be more pungent, but they are all salty and buttery in texture. Miso keeps in the refrigerator for up to a year—good to know on those cold winter nights when you crave a warm cup of the stuff.

Natto

Kids who love to play with slime, or boogers for that matter, will enjoy the stringy consistency of this ancient Japanese food. When stirred, it turns into sticky, spiderweb-like strands stretchable to infinite lengths. The nauseating aroma of *natto*, however, might be a turnoff, although a low-odor natto is available. Imagine that your dog hid a used wet diaper in a closet for a week, and you'll get an idea of how this food smells. Made from fermented soybeans, natto contains a host of beneficial ingredients including phytoestrogens, vitamin K and pyrazine, a compound proven to reduce blood clots. Companies now produce natto in bulk for the millions who have grown accustomed to this unique rice-topper, especially at breakfast time. What a way to start the day.

Kim Chee

We all know that boiled cabbage reeks, but the fermented stuff literally ambushes your olfactory nerves. A Korean staple, *kim chee*, has an unexpectedly better flavor than its scent suggests. This spicy, pickled assortment of fermented cabbage, vegetables, meat and fish was traditionally buried in the ground for weeks before it was eaten. Nowadays, a sealed jar or cellar does the trick.

WHO CUT THE CHEESE?

Speaking of fermentation, there are cheeses among the hundreds of different kinds that smell so utterly revolting, you'll want to don a gas mask. Listed here, in no particular order, are some of the most offensive.

Gorgonzola

This ripe Italian cheese has a pungent smell reminiscent of a forgotten gym bag left in a locker room over the holidays. Guaranteed to knock out the toughest football player in the NFL.

Maggot Cheese

Writhing maggots. Decomposing cheese. Put them together and you get *casu mazu*, or maggot cheese, a Sardinian delicacy and utterly shocking fusion food combining the most disgusting elements imaginable. This squishy, beige lump is so appalling that Sardinia has actually made the cheese illegal for health reasons. No surprise there—it's full of maggots, after all. Casu mazu, literally "rotten cheese," develops when the cheese fly, *Piophila casei*, is attracted to the cheese's putrid decay and lays eggs on it. The cheese quickly becomes infested with maggots, though removing the squirming larvae before eating is optional. Diners who prefer to watch them squiggle are advised to wear goggles, as the maggots have been known to practice the high jump.

Did You Know?

Cheese is made from the curdled milk of a cow, goat, buffalo, yak or almost any mammal with graspable teats. Rennet, found in the stomach lining of milk-fed calves, contains an enzyme that will separate the milk into solids (curds) and liquid (whey). Certain soft cheeses, such as cream cheese, can be made without rennet, while those mass-produced commercial blocks of cheese found in most supermarkets often use cheaper "microbial enzymes" instead of rennet. Cheese rennet (also called lady's bedstraw because it was used back in the olden days to stuff mattresses) is the name of a herb with a milk-curdling enzyme. Cheeses made with it have that characteristic creamy color from the yellow dye in its leaves and stem.

Blue Stilton

British through and through, the spidery blue veins on this crumbly hunk of odiferous cheese is actually a type of bacteria. As it ripens, the cheese is pierced with needles to allow oxygen (and the bacteria) in, which forms the veins over a three-month period.

Munster

Dubbed the "monster cheese," Munster has a truly scary scent, worse than an unwashed armpit, a St. Bernard dog's fart or a used diaper. Only the fearless dare come nose to nose with this demon cheese.

Stinking Bishop

This cheese has lived up to its barnyard-smelly title since monks first made it in the Middle Ages. Thankfully, most of the smell is from the rind, not the soft cheese, which takes up to two months to ripen. Be warned that an ungodly, odiferous mouthful can make one's breath stink to high heaven for a near-eternity.

Limburger

Hear that gagging sound? It's someone trying Limburger cheese for the first time. This *über*-stinky German cheese is wildly popular around the world, despite the fact that its acrid aroma is caused by the same bacterium that also produces the unforgettable gross, stinky-foot smell.

Époisses

This French cheese is so pungent that it has been banned from France's public transportation system because the smell permeates the vehicles, making concentration impossible. A favorite of Napoleon Bonaparte, Époisses is made from raw cow's milk and is described as being runny with frequent whiffs of ammonia.

Camembert de Normandy

Some call this unpasturized, rank cheese the only "real Camembert." A spoon is required to dig out its gooey consistency, and there is a common saying that "a ripe

Camembert squeezes like a woman's breast." Experts recommend storing this cheese upside down and ideally in a cool environment, but not in the refrigerator. Yeah, right!

Vieux Boulogne and Pont-l'Évêque

The super-stinky, soft Vieux Boulogne cheese is made in northern France. Because its rind is washed with beer, this cheese undergoes a chemical reaction that results in the equivalent of weapons of nasal destruction. Another French cheese, Pont-l'Évêque from Normandy, is also seriously smelly.

Cheese Curds

On a more pleasant cheesy note, the cheese-making process produces curds, which are solid chunks of curdled milk. The leftover liquid, or whey, usually ends up in cattle feed or protein-shake mixes, as well as ricotta, which is technically a dairy product and not a cheese. Curds are much more fun, and the freshest ones, which can be bought in the cheese section of a deli or at a farmer's market, squeak when you rub them over your teeth.

Did You Know?

Wedginald, a 44-pound round of cheddar set up on the shelf of an English cheese-making farm, was the star of a live webcam broadcast. For 12 months, some 1.7 million viewers around the world watched Wedginald mature from a young, smooth cheese into a moldy, veined one, until the celebrity dairy product was purchased by a New Zealand winery.

CHAPTER 10

Drink to This

MIND-BOGGLING BREWS

Early humans' first beverage is still the most prevalent drink on the planet. It is, of course, water, plain and simple. Whether the source is a glacier, well, river or rain barrel, we all require this hydrating liquid. For much of the world, clean water is a scarce and sought-after commodity. Those of us in developed countries merely turn on a tap, though some may be surprised to learn that their drinking water once had poop in it. Yes, super-treated sewage water purified in an advanced "toilet-to-tap" system provides safe, potable water to many cities. Others are hesitant to embrace this innovative technology, even though the crystal-clear water is better than the stuff they're already drinking.

Other beverages can also satisfy thirst. The sweet juices of ripe fruits and succulent plants were likely the second drink our ancestors collected in their cups made from hollowed-out logs and shells. Coffee and cocoa are created from special beans, and milk, the most commonly imbibed animal fluid, is so full of vitamins and minerals that it is considered more of a food than a drink. Rock paintings prove that we humans have been milking animals for thousands of years. We've also engaged in another type of beverage making—fermentation. When natural plant juices leach out and are allowed to ferment, they produce history's most famous by-product, alcohol. Clay tablets from Mesopotamia around 3500 BC show beer brewing, and even more ancient Egyptian tomb art depicts partygoers puking from too much wine. Not much has changed.

Cobra Wine

So what exactly is a cobra doing in a bottle of alcohol?
Gasping for air? Don't be alarmed—the cobra is as dead
as a doornail. The snake's energies are thought to be
absorbed into the liquid, usually a rice wine, and when
drunk provides health benefits for the body, especially
the lungs and spine. You can find almost any animal,
except perhaps fish and horses, suspended in alcohol
throughout many Asian countries. Bottled birds, mammals, reptiles, even mountain cats and small baby bears
line the shelves of traditional medicine stores like a
pickled zoo. Whatever your ailment, there's a remedy
available.

> I never drink water; that is the stuff that
> rusts pipes.
>
> – W.C. Fields

Fugu Fish-Fin Sake

Sake is well known as a Japanese wine poured into tiny cups, but there are many varieties, including fish-fin sake, made with the fins of the fugu. Yes, fugu, the infamous blowfish that can be deadly poisonous if not properly prepared. Those who try fish-fin sake will know it's the real thing if they feel an unusual tingle on the taste buds after that first sip. If not, well, the customer could complain to the staff but might be advised not to, especially if they still have the lethal fugu parts in the back kitchen.

Grog, Nog and Mead

In the 18th century, Admiral Vernon of the British Navy ordered his crew to dilute their rum. The sailors, naturally, weren't too impressed with this new rationing system. Since the admiral always wore a grogram cloak, they began to call their watery rum "grog." In colonial America, "egg 'n' grog in a noggin," or rum in a wooden cup, was shortened to eggnog, the creamy, fattening beverage synonymous with Christmastime (eggnog in French is *lait de poule* or "milk from a hen"). Another old-fashioned drink, mead, dates back at least 4000 years. Made by fermenting honey and water, mead was widely chugged by the ancient Greeks but is a challenge to find nowadays.

Ice Wine

Most fruit farmers shudder at the thought of Jack Frost chilling out their produce. Not ice wine makers. They harvest naturally frozen grapes for this rare, rich dessert wine. Freezing temperatures (17°F or −8°C) concentrate the grape juices and give ice wine its sweet, almost syrupy characteristic. You can even buy ice wine jelly to spread on your morning toast.

Kvass

Brownish, beer-like *kvass* makes swamp water look like an imported draft, but this popular, slightly fizzy beverage is sold throughout Russia, even in vending machines. Made from fermented black bread, kvass is occasionally flavored with fruit, mint or other herbs. They help cover its naturally bittersweet taste, but even kids will drink this stuff.

Mescal

Some Mexican spirits called mescals, are sold *con gusano* meaning "with a worm." The lifeless form isn't a worm at all, but rather a moth larva that makes its home on the agave (or maguey) plant. Like tequila, mescal is created from the distilled juice of the agave. Tequila, however, comes from the blue agave, and production is limited to a designated area in Mexico. Contrary to popular belief, you won't find any worms in tequila, either. Both drinks trace their origins back at least 2000 years, and the Spanish explorer Cortés described mescal as the "nectar of the gods." The idea of floating a worm in a bottled beverage is really a 50-year-old marketing gimmick, proof that the spirit has enough alcohol to pickle a juicy bug.

Pompe

The African jungle juice known as *pompe* can make people go ape. Ripe bananas (but not the squishy, black-as-coal kind) are wrapped in leaves and slowly warmed in an outdoor fire pit for several days, then peeled. The pulp is kneaded, stomped on and pressed, extracting a sweet juice that is diluted and mixed with some sorghum or other cereal flour. Once fermented, the liquid is filtered through a cotton cloth and ready to be poured into plastic bottles. Pompe, also known as *urwaga*, *lubisi* or banana beer, doesn't have an extended shelf life, but lasts long enough for most parties.

Coconut Drinks

Everyone knows that hard and hairy coconuts contain a delicious, bright white meat and flavorful oil, the essence of macaroons and piña coladas. But did you know that the sap of coconut palms is also used to make arrack, a potent Asian drink? Coconut palm wine also produces *tuba* (not the musical instrument), a type of Filipino coconut toddy. Imagine sour orange juice but 10 times stronger.

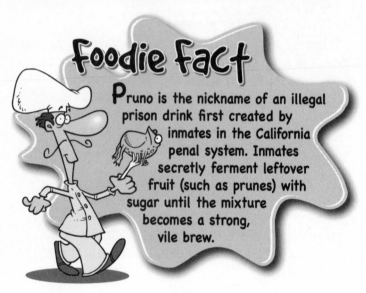

foodie fact

Pruno is the nickname of an illegal prison drink first created by inmates in the California penal system. Inmates secretly ferment leftover fruit (such as prunes) with sugar until the mixture becomes a strong, vile brew.

GOOD TO THE LAST DROP?

Asparagus Juice

Canned asparagus on the grocery shelf isn't so unusual, but what about asparagus juice? Considered a healthy and invigorating beverage in Asian countries, you can find ready-to-drink asparagus juice (recognizable by the picture of asparagus tips on the can) right beside the mango and honey royal jelly juices. It's likely no different than "normal" tomato juice, or the other vegetables, including beets, cabbage, carrots and turnips, that enthusiastic juicers squeeze the life out of. Asparagus does your body good, though it will likely make your pee stink.

Kefir

Not to be confused with a certain actor's first name, kefir is a fermented milk drink originally from the mountainous Caucasus region. The key to kefir is the whitish-yellow, living, growing mass called kefir grains. These rice- to walnut-sized lumps look like little cauliflowers but actually contain friendly live bacteria, proteins and sugars, as well as yeast. According to legend, kefir grains were given to the Orthodox people by the Prophet Mohammed. The grains are mixed with goat, cow or sheep milk, customarily in skin bags, until they reach a slightly alcoholic state of fermentation. Tangy kefir drinks initially pack a sour punch, but the taste grows on you, especially when topped with fruit or honey.

Kopi Luwak

If someone offered you the world's most expensive beverage, would you drink it? Would you still drink it if you knew that its prime ingredient came out of a cat's butt? For over 200 years, *kopi luwak* (from the Indonesia words for coffee, *kopi*, and *luwak*, which means "civet") has been the supreme leader in luxury brews, thanks to the nocturnal, cat-like palm civet. In parts of Indonesia, the civet eats red coffee cherries (the fruit of the coffee plant), which eventually pass through its digestive tract, leaving little pooped-out beans ready to be scooped. Kopi luwak connoisseurs praise the coffee's exotic, almost chocolaty richness. Knowing exactly what this expensive drink is made of, you might want to settle for an inexpensive cup of hot chocolate instead.

Lassi

In America, mention the word "lassie" and everyone thinks of a cute collie dog. In India, order a *lassi* and you're served a cold yogurt ice smoothie. Lassi can taste either salty or sweet, and is flavored with fruit, mint or even cumin. Try one if you can.

Mare's and Yak's Milk

Watch your head when you step into a yurt (a tent-like nomadic hut). There might be a leather sack full of fermenting mare's milk, or *ayrag* in Mongolian, hanging from the entrance. Anyone entering or exiting the yurt is expected to give this slightly fizzy beverage a stir. Constant mixing helps the fermentation process, but these days, most ayrag is made in plastic containers. You won't get sloshed on ayrag—it's only two percent alcohol—but the carbon dioxide in it does give the tongue a tingle. In Tibet, the female yak (the *dri* or *nak*) produces a fatty milk that is used to make yogurt and a hard, cubed, almost rancid-tasting butter often mixed with tea. Only available in Tibet, you say? Pity.

170

Urine

Who hasn't provided a doctor with a urine sample and thought, "Hey, now, that looks like apple juice"? While you may not gulp down this yellow liquid excrement, some cultures do drink animal urine for ceremonial purposes. Historically, urea, a substance found in urine, has also been used to treat skin problems such as dry skin, hives and stings. And a kind of "urine therapy," or drinking small amounts of one's own urine first thing in the morning, was thought to help cleanse the body and promote health. Then there is what used to be astronaut urine and perspiration but is now the cleanest water in space. Yes, a new system aboard NASA's space shuttle distills, filters, ionizes and oxidizes wastewater (including the fluid from showers, shaving, tooth brushing, perspiration and the water vapor inside spacesuits) into drinking water. As one astronaut says, it "turns yesterday's coffee into today's coffee."

CHAPTER 11

Palatable, Perplexing and Pukable Plants

HOW DOES YOUR GARDEN GROW?

Pity the plants. They provide us with so much—bountiful crops, useful spices, nutritious juices, idyllic scenery, not to mention oxygen—while we turn around and gobble them up. They may be at the bottom of the food chain, but no meal is complete without a plant on the plate. Colorful vegetables and luscious fruits add variety and vitamins to our diet. Nature's almost endless plant collection contains some of the most unusual living things on earth. There are plants that stink to high heaven (the corpse flower smells like rotting flesh), others that are carnivorous (ever see a Venus fly trap?) and a few that actually resemble huge genitalia. Even more surprising are the weird plants that people willingly devour. The devil's tongue, for instance, is unmistakably phallic, and Victorian ladies were shielded from viewing its suggestive shape. Its tubers, however, are quite edible and have provided starch to Asian diets for over 2000 years. The moral: Don't judge a plant by its appearance; it's the taste that counts. Right?

Argan Oil

This nutty oil derives from the kernels of Morocco's spiny argan tree—and it's veritable liquid gold. Used in cooking and cosmetics (argan oil is believed to have anti-aging properties), this oil doesn't come cheap. The highest quality kind is traditionally collected by hand, or rather, by goat. It's the goats that climb the argan tree, eat its fruit and poop out the pits containing the kernels. Local women use stones to grind these kernels into a brownish paste, and then knead it by hand to extract the oil. One wonders if they know how much female shoppers in rich countries pay for creams containing their precious oil.

> Do vegetarians eat animal crackers?
> – Unknown

Cattails

If, by chance, you find yourself stranded in the swampy wilds, look for the fuzzy brown tops of cattails. These slender, marsh-loving plants are your meal ticket. In the spring or summer, nibble on the raw tips or on the white tender stems. The green flower heads can also be eaten like raw corn on the cob. In the fall, use the yellow pollen as a flour to thicken soups, or mash the roots into a useful starch. After you're rescued, become one of those wild-food foragers and enjoy cattail cuisine all year long.

Colored Potatoes

Imagine blue French fries, blue mashed potatoes, blue potato salad—all courtesy of the blue potato. Or why not celebrate the festive season with the candy cane potato, named for its oblong shape, cream-colored flesh and a red ring just below its reddish skin? Other kooky tubers include the fingerling potato, which resembles a fat finger, and the Russian banana potato, with an appearance that could easily confuse a monkey. Swanky spuds, indeed.

Chili Peppers

There exists on this planet a chili pepper so out of the ordinary, so fiery hot, that it's the culinary equivalent of an atomic bomb. Chili love burns when it comes to the Bhut Jolokia of northern India. This little pepper has

Talk about playing with food. The instruments of the unique Vienna Vegetable Orchestra are made entirely of—you guessed it—vegetables! Pumpkins turn into drums, hollowed out carrots become flutes, rubbed cabbages squeak and eggplants are clapped together like long purple cymbals. After each performance, the musicians serve the audience fresh vegetable soup from the leftover vegetables that didn't make the cut.

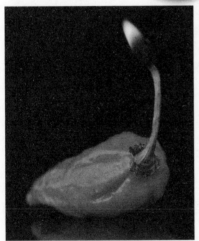

earned a reputation as the "ghost chili" among locals because anyone who eats one will likely end up leaving his or her physical body. The *Guinness Book of World Records* rates it as the spiciest chili on earth using Scoville Heat Units (SHU), a measurement of how "hot" a pepper can get. Blame this "heat" on a colorless, flavorless chemical compound called capsaicin, which is found in super-high concentrations in the membranes surrounding a chili pepper's seeds. A regular supermarket bell pepper rates 0 SHU, while an average *jalapeño* is approximately 5000 SHU. By comparison, the former heavyweight of blazing heat, the Red Savina *habañero* measures 577,000 SHU, which makes swallowing a bucket of lit cigarette butts feel like a frozen slushie. The Bhut Jolokia, however, is almost twice as hot, with a staggering hellfire rating of 1,001,304 SHU.

Fiddleheads

Squint hard enough and, yes, those tight, green, curly vegetables on the dinner plate do look somewhat like the curve of a fiddle. Fiddleheads are the immature leaves of the ostrich fern. Steamed or boiled and brushed with melted butter, they're absolute music to your mouth.

Did You Know?

"**H**unan hand" and "jalapeño eye" are slang terms for chemical burns on the skin or in the eye from capsaicin. If you do ingest too much spice, put out the chili fire with milk or any dairy product as soon as possible. In a pinch, cucumber, bread or sugar will also help.

Flowers

They're elegant in vases and bouquets, but gourmet chefs know that flowers are more than just pretty plant parts. Their elegant and colorful petals turn an ordinary salad or dessert into a pièce de résistance, and not just to rabbits. These blooms aren't meant to be picked out, or over, but instead savored like delicate, well, flowers. From peonies to primroses, edible flowers have been used in cooking and decoration for centuries. The ancient *Apicius* cookbook also includes a recipe for "brains with rose petals." Taste a pansy and discover a subtle hint of grape or mint, or try cornflower and bachelor's buttons (they can also be mashed to make an edible food coloring). Bright orange, red or yellow nasturtium flowers and leaves add spice; even Dwight Eisenhower, the former U.S. president, enjoyed them in his vegetable soup.

PALATABLE, PERPLEXING and PUKABLE PLANTS

Grass Jelly

This blackish, well-liked Asian product does not come from lawnmower mulch. Also called leaf or herbal jelly, grass jelly is made by boiling the leaves and stalks of a plant from the mint family. Sold in cans, the slightly bitter grass jelly can be eaten alone or mixed with fruit and milk to make a sweet drink considered "yin" or "cooling" on a hot day. Very groovy.

Hemp

First, a disclaimer—this is about hemp, not the marijuana plant. While industrial hemp and marijuana both come from the *Cannabis* genus, the level of psychoactive ingredient (THC) in industrial hemp is so low, you could smoke 100 acres and still not get high. Next to tobacco, hemp was once the most popular agricultural crop in the U.S. Strong and versatile, the plant was used for almost everything from rope to clothing to food and oil. Nutritious hempseeds are full of fiber and essential fatty acids and can be used whole in baking or ground into a hemp powder for cakes and cookies. Colonial Virginia of the 17th century even required farmers to grow this useful plant. Today, a crop ban by the Drug Enforcement Association means that hemp cannot usually be grown legally in the U.S., though some farmers are currently challenging this law. Hemp is, however, widely cultivated in Canada, China and many other countries without any problems. Go figure.

Prickly Pear Cactus

Estimates are that cacti have been a part of the human diet for over 9000 years. No doubt, the first swear word is equally as old. One can imagine the expletives uttered by the original unlucky individual who first tried to harvest these spiky plants with bare hands. For instance, the most common edible cactus, the prickly pear, is deliciously succulent, but you have to get by its needle-like spines first. That's not all. The oval, paddle-shaped pads, known as *nopales*, are also covered in miniscule, hair-like prickles called glochids. Without thick gloves, they can get under your skin in the worst way. Don't even try to lick them off, as they mercilessly burrow into human tongues, too. Nevertheless, nopales remain a popular vegetable in Mexico and Central America. Look for the firm, light green cacti—the larger, thicker ones are older and have extra-gluey juice and a stringier texture. Cut, peel or burn the prickles off before they get under your skin. Nopales pads are best boiled a couple of times before preparation, as this helps get rid of the sliminess. The pads thicken stews and soups, and cactus juice can be made into jelly or wine. Crunchy cacti have a tart, green-bean taste and can be eaten raw, roasted, pickled, candied, steamed or cooked with eggs in a skillet to create a Southwestern-style omelet.

foodie fact

Another name for okra is "lady's fingers," in reference to its long, thin, dainty, finger-like appearance. Okra pods contain creamy, edible seeds and as well as a sticky substance with thickening properties.

PALATABLE, PERPLEXING and PUKABLE PLANTS

The prickly pear was introduced to Australia in 1839 as a food source and a hedge for cattle. It spread so invasively that some 60 million acres were taken over in less than 100 years. Only the import of a cactus-eating caterpillar finally curbed the cactus invasion.

Spirulina

The ancient Aztecs knew that the blue-green froth that floated on their inland lakes was a good source of food. They harvested, dried and made bread out of these single-celled algae, which they called *tecuitlatl*, or "excrement of stone," because the algae often grew on rocks. Back in the 1970s, spirulina was touted as the superfood of the future by the United Nations. NASA even considered its cultivation for long-term space missions. Fresh spirulina may look like the scum scraped off an old shower curtain, but it is stacked with nutrients, including over 60 percent protein and significant amounts of vitamins A, E and B12 and essential amino acids. Although it is still produced today, most spirulina ends up as an expensive nutritional supplement for the wealthy and not the magic solution to world hunger. Perhaps one day, this algae will make a comeback and combat malnourished millions. After all, legend has it that a type of spirulina may have been the biblical "manna" that appeared on the ground and saved Moses' Israelites from starvation in the desert.

Stinging Nettle

The next time you tumble into a nettle patch or step on one of these prickly weeds, don't curse the plant. Tell yourself, "Nettle tastes great." It may take several dozen repetitions (at least until the itchy rash disappears), but you might just convince yourself to try some of the many nettle dishes available, including nettle tea, nettle cheese, nettle beer and the ever-popular nettle soup. Yes, this member of the mint family has been a culinary classic for centuries. While its stinging, needle-like hairs successfully help the nettle protect itself from grazing animals, its front-line of defense disappears when cooked. Boiled, steamed or sautéed, nettle transforms into a benign, spinach-like green full of calcium, magnesium and iron. Nettles are nice—but only on a plate.

Tree Bark

Fruits are not the only nutritious products trees provide. Certain edible tree barks and gums contain starch and sugars, as well as calcium and magnesium, which can stave off hunger for a lost forest wanderer. It's not the crusty outer bark that's eaten, but rather the cambium directly underneath it through which sap travels. Indigenous peoples of North America scraped pliable strips off pines, spruces and other tree varieties and ate them fresh or baked. They were careful not to peel around the whole tree and cut only enough to leave a scar. If you think bark vittles are only for tree huggers, check your spice rack. True cinnamon sticks come from the inner bark of Asian evergreen *Cinnamommus* trees, a little something to mull over while you sip your next hot cider.

Weeds

Wild and formerly unwanted plants are making a comeback on the dinner table. Best of all, they're available at a vacant (and, hopefully, pesticide-free) lot near you. These include—but are definitely not limited to—garlic mustard (a favorite of Europeans during the 1800s), shepherd's purse, wild spinach and even Queen Anne's lace, also known as wild carrot because the root smells like, you guessed it, a carrot. Also popular is the ubiquitous dandelion, from the French term *dent de lion*, which means "lion's tooth" (according to the French, the leaves resemble lion's teeth). The fresh, young leaves, not the bitter older ones, are best picked in early spring and make excellent salad greens. The flowers can be fermented into dandelion wine and, when dried, those infamous roots make a satisfying coffee substitute similar to chicory. Be careful when digging these babies out of the ground. Dandelion roots have been known to grow up to a monstrous five feet deep. So the next time a neighbor complains about your weedy lawn, simply tell him you are growing an alternative garden, and then invite him in for a glass of vintage dandelion wine.

Soy

Soybeans have been cultivated in Asian countries for over 4000 years but didn't catch on in the West until the 1960s. While most of us now buy soy sauce along with ketchup and other condiments, the real Chinese kind has far less salt than our westernized supermarket brands. Nevertheless, it's now much easier to find new soybean products in North America and Europe than ever before. Take edamame, for example, which are immature green soybeans. Snack on dried, salted ones instead of peanuts—they're good for you, too, because like all soy, they contain isoflavonoids renowned for their health benefits. In Beijing, you can buy a pastry made of soybean flour called *ludagun*, which dates back to ancient times. Just make sure the one you eat is no more than a few days old.

Textured Vegetable Protein

Defatted soy flour, also known as textured vegetable protein (TVP), is the dry, granular stuff next to the organic flour in the health-food store. It's also sold preformed into replica chicken nuggets or hamburger patties. Sprinkle the dry, crumbly kind into chili instead of ground beef, or grab a TVP burger and cover it with condiments. Odds are these low-fat and better-for-you meat substitutes will be almost indistinguishable from the real thing.

Tofu

A recent revival of interest in soybean curd suggests
that this nutritious substance may have finally ditched
its reputation as a hippy commune food. It's about time,
too, since soybean cultivation dates back thousands of
years. One of the soybean's best prodigies is tofu, the
product made from curdled hot soymilk that is pressed
and formed into cubes. By itself, tofu hardly has any
flavor, but it can be sweetened or spiced, and eaten a
million different ways. There's soft, silken, dried or firm
tofu and even a hard, smoked tofu described as having
a taste similar to Gouda cheese. Tofu has also enabled
vegetarians to fully join in holiday dinners with their own
ball-shaped "tofu turkey." Okay, it doesn't have wings or
drumsticks, but this creative meal-in-a-box does come
with dumplings, a bag of cranberry sauce and even two
tofu-jerky wishbones.

Yuba

Boil a saucepan of milk, and a thin, floating layer usually
forms on the surface. The same thing happens to boiled
soybeans, but don't throw this filmy substance down
the drain. It can be made into delicate bean curd sheets
known as "tofu skin" or *yuba*. Sold dried, yuba is reconsti-
tuted and used to wrap dim sum items such as yuba rolls,
or it can be cut up into yummy yuba noodles.

MAGIC MUSHROOMS

Dancing Mushrooms

The Japanese maitake, or dancing mushrooms, are also called "dancing butterflies" and "hen of the woods" because they look either like fan-carrying Japanese dancers, fluttering butterflies or chicken tail feathers. Another explanation is that mushroom harvesters are so ecstatic when they discover this light gray fungus that they break into a happy dance. The petal-like caps of these mushrooms have a mellow, nutty taste and can be baked, stuffed or dried to make a tea. According to mycologists (mushroom experts), most can be found near decaying things, such as at the base of a dead tree.

Giant Puffball

Colossal, round, white balls appear in the middle of lush lawns and fertile forests. They're not mushrooms on steroids, but rather super-sized fungi called giant puffballs. Many are easily the size of a bald man's head, and the largest can reach nearly 50 pounds. When tapped, an edible puffball should sound like an inflated football, but stay away from the yellow, brown, greenish or hairy ones (or risk a terrible tummy ache). Peel away the tough skin first, then slice, dice and fry it in butter. If your puffball weighed anywhere near the world-record holder—over 48 pounds—be prepared for leftovers.

Truffles

Lumpy underground fungus is worth more than you think. Much more. At one charity auction, a white truffle (and we're not talking chocolate dainties here) fetched over $300,000. While you may not have to mortgage your house for a handful of regular truffles, these black, brown, gray or white mushrooms remain a luxury item. The ancient Egyptians cooked them in goose fat, but today they can be bought whole or canned, ready to be shaved raw into dishes or used as an exquisite, earthy-tasting stuffing. Another option is gourmet truffle oil, but watch out for brands spiked with synthetic flavors to cut costs. Of the 70 truffle varieties, almost half are from Europe, though deforestation and pesticide use have made these pricy fungal treasures harder to find.

Part of the reason that truffles are so expensive is the way they are collected. Truffles contain a chemical similar to one found in a male pig's saliva, which is why female pigs, or "truffle hogs," eagerly root around for them. The pigs, however, like to eat the truffles they dig up, so nowadays, dogs are the preferred truffle hounds. Incidentally, that chemical truffle scent is also found in men's underarms. Males reading this book are advised to wear deodorant if they plan on being close to any female pigs.

Other Wacky Mushroom Names
Oyster
Shaggy cap
Ink cap
Elf-cup
Shiitake
Lawyer's wig

Did You Know?
Eating fungus is called mycophagy.

Tree Ear Mushroom

If a tree falls in the forest, does anyone hear it fall? Maybe the tree ear mushroom does. Tree ears—not to be confused with a rugby player's cauliflower ear—are one of a variety of mushrooms known under many names including Jew's ear, ear of Judas, wood ear and cloud's ear. They do grow on the sides of tree trunks and, yes, they somewhat resemble giant, brown, gummy ears, but when dried, the tree ear mushrooms shrink and darken into an unrecognizable mass. Crumbled into sauces or stews for added texture, the mushrooms rehydrate easily and have been a principle ingredient in traditional Asian cooking for centuries.

Trivia Tidbit

One small Michigan town celebrates its annual Humungus Fungus festival in honor of the humble mushroom and the fact that the state is home to the world's oldest living organism, a 38-acre fungus that could be thousands of years old.

PALATABLE, PERPLEXING and PUKABLE PLANTS

Stinkhorn

Its proper name is *Phallaceae* and that pretty well sums up what this freaky but common mushroom resembles—a part of the male anatomy. The stinkhorn is an erect, slimy fungus with spores on its cap. But wait, visually is not the only way this mushroom offends. The smell it gives off is so disgustingly vile that it attracts flies like decaying meat. These bugs congregate on the sticky tip, inadvertently spreading spores and thereby helping to propagate baby stinkhorns that keep the reek alive. Fresh stinkhorns are way too stinky for most people, so they're sold dehydrated. Thankfully, adding water doesn't bring back their repulsive odor.

Did You Know?

Prized as royal fare in ancient Egypt, mushrooms only became popular in the United States during the 19th century. Flavorful and edible, the mushroom remains an important ingredient in vegetarian dishes and is known in Asia as the "meat without bones."

Huitalacoche

Corn smut. Now there's something you can't wait to see on your plate. In Canada and the U.S., this corn fungus is the bane of farmers, but to the Mexicans, *huitalacoche* is part of their food culture. Its name comes from a word meaning "raven's excrement," and not surprisingly, this ugly, gray-black fungus does resemble a huge wad of bird poop, likely from a pterodactyl. Also known as "Mexican truffle," huitalacoche grows on corn right before harvest time. Fresh or canned, it can be served in a sauce or as a side dish and has a sweet, smoky flavor. Once you're hooked on the huitalacoche, try it as a mescal in a "mushroom margarita."

Rock Guts

Leave it to the nature-savvy Aboriginal peoples to save the early voyageurs from starvation. They showed the ill-prepared Europeans where to find food when nothing else was available. One such source was lichen, a hard, green or black, fungal plant that can be scraped off forest rocks, then washed and boiled as a broth thickener. It's also called rock tripe (*tripe de roche*), which roughly translates from French as "rock guts." One 18th-century explorer described this mossy meal as "palatable" and "generally most esteemed when boiled in fish-liquor."

FUNKY AND FEARSOME FRUIT

Alligator Pear

Chances are you've seen, and have probably eaten, an
alligator pear. It's green with a rough, leather-like skin
and grows in the same regions alligators live. Centuries
ago, the Spaniards may have mispronounced the Nahuatl
word for the fruit, *ahuacatl*. Yes, the alligator pear is simply another name for the ordinary avocado.

Betel Nut

Chew. Chew. Spit. Repeat. That's what countless betel nut
chewers around the world do all day, every day. Wrapped
in betel pepper leaves and sprinkled with a dash of lime,
the nut of the betel palm is responsible for this mastica-
tory pleasure par excellence. Unfortunately, betel nut
chewing has also been linked to oral cancer, but that fact
doesn't stop avid betel nut fans—they're addicted.

Breadfruit

This bumpy, starchy, South Pacific fruit is cooked like
a vegetable, has the texture of an eggplant and, when
unripe, tastes like bread. William Bligh, the commander
of the late-18th-century ship, the HMS *Bounty*, had the
task of bringing young breadfruit trees from Polynesia to
the Caribbean as a cheap food source for slaves. While in
Tahiti, many of his crew grew accustomed to the pleasant
island life and didn't want to leave. For this, and other

reasons, the crew decided to take matters into their own hands. The outcome? Mutiny on the *Bounty*. Ironically, when another ship collected and successfully transplanted the breadfruit to the West Indies years later, the slaves refused to eat it.

Bush Coconut

Note: This is bush tucker food, not regular grocery store fare, and the bush coconut isn't a coconut or even a nut. It's the home of a legless, wingless, female insect called a coccid. This insect lives off the sap of the Australian bloodwood tree and builds her golf-ball-sized home on its branches. Native Aborigines knock the bush coconuts down, crack them open, drink the refreshing fluid and eat the juicy grub inside.

Candle and Sausage Trees

Believe it or not, candles and sausages do grow on trees. In the tropical climates of Central and South America, the candle tree, *Parmentiera cereifera*, produces hanging, yellow fruit shaped like long taper candles. What's more, the fruit gives off a slight apple scent, similar to that of those fancy green-apple-perfumed candles you can buy in home decorating shops.

In South Africa, the mature brown fruit of the sausage tree, *Kigelia pinnata*, dangles like huge, two-foot-long frankfurters. Inside is a fleshy, but definitely not beef-, pork- or chicken-flavored, seed-filled pulp.

Dishcloth Gourd

What do a dishcloth gourd and a loofah have in common? Believe it or not, they're one and the same. That's right, the foot-long dishcloth gourd fruit has a spongy-textured interior known as a loofah. In the early 20th century, the loofah was used as a filter in ship boilers or as insulation. Who would have guessed?

Dragon Fruit

The dragon fruit, or *pitahaya* (*pitaya*), sounds like terrifying produce, but its appearance isn't that hideous. This succulent fruit can be found in almost any supermarket, and most are imported from Vietnam, Thailand or southern Mexico. It starts off as the large, white, night-blooming flower of the climbing cactus and ripens into a softball-sized fruit with a thick, red or yellow skin. The orange-tinged flesh of the yellow dragon fruit has more flavor than its pink cousin and tastes like a cross between a kiwi, a melon and a gooseberry. Spoon the fruit out and enjoy, but watch out for the hundreds of tiny seeds that get stuck between your teeth.

Durian

Imagine a fruit so sickeningly smelly that it has been banned in many Southeast Asian airports and hospitals. On the outside, durian vaguely resembles a medieval

mace, but inside is a luscious, creamy, pale yellow pulp. Millions of people worldwide describe the spiky, football-sized durian as the fruit that "smells like hell but tastes like heaven." Its velvety, custard-like flesh unfortunately deteriorates quickly, turning the durian's hidden fragrant grapefruit overtones into the overpowering stench of a rotting bog full of dirty socks. When unripe, and not as stinky, it can be cooked as a vegetable or made into a sweet paste. Other durian delights include thin, fried durian chips, durian cookies, durian candy and scrumptious durian ice cream.

Ebe or Eben

To members of the UFO community, the term EBE stands for "extraterrestrial biological entity." To the rest of the world, ebe is a purple, thumb-sized fruit found in Nigeria. Locals suck out its tart, green flesh as a juicy treat. Maybe EBE aliens do, too.

Filbert

That chocolate bar may contain a filbert filling. Huh? Filbert is another term for the scrumptious hazelnut. Hazelnut trees can produce fruit for hundreds of years. Not only can you crack open a hazelnut and eat it raw, but this little nut also provides a delectable oil. The ancient Greek physician, Dioscorides, even wrote that mashed filbert shells applied to the scalp could cure baldness. The name filbert may have been coined by the 7th-century monk, St. Philibert, whose feast day is August 20, when there are tons of nuts lying around.

PALATABLE, PERPLEXING and PUKABLE PLANTS

Fuzzy Melon

This hairy melon, or fuzzy squash, has a cucumber-like flavor, green skin and a fine, hairy, velvety texture. As it ripens, the hair disappears, just like that of more than a few middle-aged men.

Horned Melon

Watch out for armored melons. Africa's horned melon is no exception, and its spikes can cause damage to un-gloved hands. This orange fruit, which is also now found in Australia, has another, less fearsome name—the jelly melon. Yes, inside the tough-as-nails horned melon is a yellow-green, jelly-like flesh with a taste somewhere be-tween that of a cucumber and a lime.

Ice Cream Bean

If the kids won't eat their veggies, try the ice cream bean. Okay, it's not a vegetable, it's the fruit of a tropical tree, but it does hang in three-foot-long pods that look like beans that have been cultivated next to a nuclear power plant. Inside each pod are oversized seeds covered with a sweet, white pulp that purportedly tastes exactly like vanilla ice cream. Best eaten fresh, the ripe ice cream bean is a favorite pecking treat for birds, even those without a sugar cone.

More Beans, Please! A Samplng of Weird Bean Names (Besides the regular kidney bean)
Appaloosa bean (black and white, like its pony
    namesake)
Asparagus bean
Black turtle bean
Butter bean
Calypso beans (or yin yang bean or orca bean)
Christmas or chestnut bean (that taste a little like chest-
    nuts when cooked)

Cranberry bean
Egyptian bean
Eye of goat bean
European soldier bean
Fava bean
Hyacinth bean
Jacob's cattle bean
Leather britches bean
Mortgage runner bean
Rattlesnake bean (the pods twist like snakes on the vines)
Tongues of fire bean (won't burn your tongue)
Trout bean
Velvet bean

> Beans, beans, the musical fruit. The more you eat the more you toot!
>
> – Children's rhyme

Jackfruit

We're used to seeing fruit dangling from branches, but the jackfruit grows out of the tree trunk, measures up to three feet long and weighs 100 pounds. The jackfruit does double duty. Unripe, it's a vegetable, but it matures into a fruit. Ripe jackfruits have a tendency to reek of rotten onions, but inside they're as sweet as pineapple, with a few hundred, inch-long seeds. These seeds can even be roasted like chestnuts. Look for canned jackfruit in international supermarkets.

Did You Know?

Jujube candies originally contained juice from the fruit of the jujube plant.

Jujube

Jujubes aren't just chewy fruity candies at the bulk store. A jujube is actually an Asian shrub that produces a small, dark red, oval fruit about one or two inches long. The fruit has an apple-prune taste and once ripe, wrinkles quickly to become the Chinese date, a favorite in China for 4000 years. Jujube can be also be made into a tea, wine or syrup, but perhaps melting down a saucepan full of the candies will get the same result.

Kumquat

The late comedian, George Carlin, once said that the kumquat had the funniest name of all. These peculiar fruits don't exactly look normal, either. In fact, they could pass as tiny, orange footballs for elves. Fortunately, the kumquat's outer layer isn't pigskin tough and doesn't need to be peeled. It actually tastes sweet compared to the tart flesh inside. The kumquat makes a great marmalade and has been crossed with other citrus to produce new fruits with equally amusing names such as the orangquat and limequat.

Lucmo

Cooler North American regions may have their own golden delicious maple syrup, but South America goes one better with *lucmo* (also called *lucuma*), known in Peru as the "gold of the Incas." Bite into this oval, brownish fruit, and you'll swear it's been drizzled in maple syrup. The firm yellow pulp of the lucmo can be made into juice, stewed fruit or jam. When dried into a powder, it blends well into in pastries, puddings, baby food and ice creams. Now that's a maple syrup fruit.

Mangosteen

Unlike the familiar mango, the mangosteen, which comes from the slow-growing, tropical mangosteen tree, is smallish and round with a deep purple skin. Inside, each mangosteen has a white, billiard-ball-sized pulp described by one 19th-century explorer as having a taste "which nobody can describe." Queen Victoria purportedly deemed it her favorite fruit and offered a reward to anyone who could bring her an unspoiled one from the Indies.

Mangosteen sections like an orange, but is more slippery than a sliver of wet soap and possesses a sweet tang similar to a mild kiwi. Cut around the fruit's middle or "equator," twist, then pry open to reveal the chubby, whitish flesh. This heavenly little fruit can also be purchased canned or frozen, but if you do eat it raw, watch out for the dark juice that oozes out from under the mangosteen's skin, as it stains fingers and fabrics a deep purple.

Miracle Fruit

When eaten, this small, red, African berry truly turns into a miracle fruit. It has the inimitable characteristic of being able to make anything bitter or sour taste sweet. The miracle fruit contains a special protein that coats taste buds and performs this taste-test marvel. Now if it could only make broccoli taste exactly like candy.

Monkey Bread

Monkey bread (not to be confused with the sweet-dough loaf of the same name) is the fruit of one of the largest trees in the world, the African baobab tree. The baobab can live 1000 years or more, and its dried leaves are also edible. Its fruit resembles a large gourd and can be ground into flour. The pulp of fresh monkey bread fruit also makes a thirst-quenching beverage. One monkey bread drink to go, please!

Quince

What if Eve didn't hand Adam an apple, but rather a quince? A what? This ancient, Old World fruit can be described as a cross between a lumpy apple and a yellow pear with the fuzz of a peach. Freshly picked quince gives off a heavenly perfume scent, but eaten raw, it tastes like a thousand sour grapes. No wonder quince is thought to be the legendary forbidden fruit offered by Eve. Once Adam took a bite, he probably regretted his decision. Perhaps Eve should have used her newfound knowledge to cook quince and its natural pectin into a delicious jelly preserve instead.

Tree Tomato

This reddish, egg-shaped fruit looks likes a tomato, cooks like a tomato and has the same flavor as an unripe tomato, but grows on a tree. Although native to South America, the tree tomato crops up worldwide. In 1967, New Zealanders changed the name from "tree tomato" to "tamarillo" because they thought it had a nicer ring to it and eliminated any confusion with its more popular cousin.

Yucca

Think of yucca as the other potato. This desert plant with a long, brown taproot is also known as the Spanish bayonet, but it's a vegetable through and through. Stuff it with cheese, dice it into soups or slice and fry it to make a sort of yucca French fries side dish. Even the flower can be eaten, either raw or steamed, from the edible and definitely not yucky yucca.

CHAPTER 12

Odds 'n' Ends

BACK TO BASICS

Some questions beg for an answer. Why are edible oil products in the grocery dairy section? Is processed food actually fake food? If I eat a pile of dirt, have I had my daily mineral quotient? It's hard to know where some foods, and food additives, fit in the supermarket of life. Take honey, for example. This sweet stuff has been around forever but is derived from an unusual source, bees. Honey doesn't spoil quickly, either, which brings us to another question. Why do some foods last longer than others, and why is the best before date on a carton of milk or loaf of white bread often light years in the future? In a word, preservatives. Yes, much of what we buy has been pumped full of the edible equivalent of anti-aging products. It's nothing new. Humans have strived to better preserve food ever since the sun introduced dried fruit and snow gave us frozen entrées. Since then, we've developed canned goods, instant mashed potatoes, packaged noodles and more. And that fruit or vegetable sitting on the produce table may not be 100 percent fruit and nothing else. It is likely covered in a wax such as the plant-derived carnauba or candellia wax, or an insect-based shellac. Don't worry—waxes have been used on, and in, foods since the 1920s. If you don't like it on your apple, wash it off. On the other hand, if it's a genetically altered apple, rearranging its DNA over the kitchen sink is an impossible task. Food-related questions can be endless. What's eating you?

Pablum

Its name comes from the Latin word *pabulum*, which means "animal feed," and while you could feed it to your pets, it wasn't meant for them. Pablum is a precooked, easy-to-digest infant cereal loaded with vitamins and minerals. Developed in 1930 by three Canadian doctors, pablum was formulated to help prevent infant malnutrition. Think of it as the baby food equivalent of a three-course dinner with a protein shake to boot. Pablum has since been fed to millions of babies, despite its rather bland taste.

> As a child, my family's menus consisted of two choices: take it or leave it.
> – Buddy Hackett

Carmine

Is your food bugged? To find out, check the ingredients. If "natural color" or "cochineal extract" is listed, yes, it definitely contains bugs. Carmine, carminic acid and cochineal products add red or pink coloring to foods such as raspberry ice cream, yogurt, fake crab flakes and even maraschino cherries. These color additives are considered all-natural because they're derived from the crushed up bodies of an insect, the cochineal beetle, and have been safely used in foods for decades. Vegetarians and those who don't eat insects for religious or other reasons might want to pass on anything with carmine or cochineal extract. The rest of us can try not to think of the pulverized beetles in our strawberry milkshakes.

Chewing Gum

Five thousand years ago, one of our ancient ancestors chewed a hunk of birch tar and then looked for a bedpost to stick it on overnight. Not being able to find one (furniture hadn't yet been invented), he or she spat it out. There it remained for millennia until modern-day archaeologists unearthed it and agreed that, yes, this tooth-marked birch tar remnant was the world's oldest chewing gum. Prehistoric humans may have used birch tar for its antiseptic properties, and Native peoples did the same with spruce tree resin, but we chew gum out of habit, to freshen breath and because it tastes good. Chewing gum was first manufactured in the 1800s, often with the natural gum resin of a tropical evergreen tree, chicle. Now doesn't "chicle" sound like it would make a great name for a brand of chewing gum?

Chuño

In the early 16th century, Spanish conquistadors trekked through the Andes on their quest for New World domination. Conquering cultures was hard work and naturally made them hungry. So what was available to eat? Local foodstuffs, of course, including a funny, shriveled-up, mummified former potato called a *chuño*. To understand exactly what a chuño is, leave a potato out overnight in the cold, dry, Andean climate. It will essentially transform into a freeze-dried potato, a chuño, which is still a popular South American food. The centuries old chuño-making method involves drying potatoes in the sun, then trampling on them to squeeze out any remaining liquid. This process continues for about a week (some are washed and become white chuños), and the result is a tough but very portable food item that can keep for months and even years—a chewy chuño.

Gelatin

Those wiggly and jiggly jelly desserts contain gelatin, a colorless, odorless substance. When mixed with liquids, it's the gelatin that makes them set in fancy molds. What might dampen your desire for jelly is where gelatin comes from—the boiled-down bones and cartilage of cows, pigs and other butchered animals. The process produces collagen, which is later dried and ground to a powder, and then packaged as gelatin. If simmered animal bones don't sound too appealing, gelatin can also be extracted from certain algae. The choice is yours.

Marmite and Vegemite

Who would have thought that dark brown, sticky, toast and sandwich spreads would be so popular? Both Marmite and its Down Under counterpart, Vegemite (actually owned by the Kraft company), are salty yeast extracts. They aren't too bad for you, either, and are chock full of B vitamins and safe for vegetarians. So which one wins the taste test? The original Marmite is over 100 years old. The word "marmite" refers to a French cooking pot similar to the one on the jar of Marmite. Vegemite has a pastier, less runny texture with a slightly paler appearance. Both have a bitter, salty taste. Pop a beef bouillon cube into your mouth and you'll get the idea. Both should

be spread thinly on bread or crackers, but be warned—
they tend to be addictive. The more you eat these products, the thicker you tend to spread them. Now *that's*
great marketing.

Honey

Honey isn't weird, or is it? Remember, this is puked up
nectar. Yes, most of us have a jar of bee vomit—okay, bee
spit sounds better—in the pantry, but do we realize how
much hard insect labor is involved in the production of
this golden liquid? Busy worker bees must visit about
two million flowers and fly the equivalent distance of
more than twice around the world to make one pound of
honey. Each bee sucks up the nectar and stores it in one
of its two stomachs, called the "honey stomach." When
the stomach is full, the bee returns to the hive, where it
passes the nectar back and forth to other bees—yes, they
buzz around and share the regurgitation. This perpetual
puke-passing party partially digests the nectar until it
is stored in the honeycomb. Constant fanning from the
bees' wings helps to eventually evaporate the liquid into
nature's sweetest syrupy throw-up, honey.

Hamburger Ice Cream

As the song goes, "I scream, you scream, we all scream
for ice cream." There are, however, some truly shriek-
able, frightening flavors out there. Take hamburger ice
cream, a dairy product infused with bits of meat, cheese
and French fries. It's just one of the more than 800
different kinds available at a famous Venezuelan ice
cream parlor. The owner says he uses only natural ingredients in his ice cream mixtures, which include onion,
cola, hot dog, rose, fried pork rind, asparagus, garlic and
spaghetti bolognese. Unusual ice creams can be found all
over the world. One Taiwanese ice cream company has an
entire seafood line (I'll have a scoop of cuttlefish and two
of mango seaweed, please), while Great Britain touts a

rather stinky Stilton ice cream. The Japanese, however, seemed to have cornered the market when it comes to crazy flavors. Wasabi, miso and tomato sound downright tame next to squid ink, chicken wing or the nay-able raw horseflesh (*basashi*) ice cream.

Salt Licorice

It looks, smells and feels like an ordinary black licorice candy. Don't be fooled. Try one and you'll swear someone just poured a pound of salt into your mouth. Surprisingly, there isn't even a pinch of sodium chloride, or table salt, in salt licorice. What it does contain is ammonium chloride, which tastes like regular salt. This hard candy is a favorite in Scandinavian and Baltic countries. In Finland, it's known as *salmiakki* or *salmiak* candy, from the Latin root word for ammonium chloride. If you can't get used to the flavor, give it as a special salty treat to your pet. Especially if your pet happens to be a cow.

Did You Know?
The compound glycyrrhizin is found in licorice root and is 50 times sweeter than sugar.

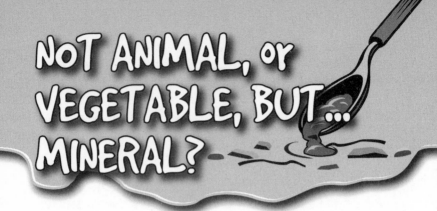

NOT ANIMAL, or VEGETABLE, BUT... MINERAL?

Pica

This disorder gives a whole new meaning to the phrase "eat dirt." While small children often shove anything in their mouths, a person with pica compulsively eats non-food objects such as paper, paint chips, metal or plastic. The term "pica" comes from the Latin word for magpie, a bird reputed to eat almost anything. Pregnant woman have been known to crave coal or other minerals, and this may be related to anemia or iron and zinc deficiencies.

Some cases are mild, but the more severe ones can involve the consumption of soap, forks and even toothbrushes. Either way, pica patients require psychological help and often medical intervention.

In one 1927 case, a 42-year-old woman had surgery to remove over 2500 objects from her stomach, including 1000 bent metal pins. In 2004, a 62-year-old French man with a history of psychiatric illness complained of stomach pains. Doctors soon discovered through X-ray that he had consumed 350 coins, as well as several necklaces and needles. He required immediate surgery but unfortunately died shortly afterwards from complications. So if a friend starts aggressively biting a spoon, please take him or her to a doctor! It could be pica, and friends don't let friends eat the cutlery.

Extreme Indigestion

Hyalophagia: consumption of glass

Geophagy: consumption of chalk, clay or soil

Pagophagia: consumption of ice

Coniophagia: consumption of dust

Xylophagia: consumption of wood

Trichophagia: consumption of hair

Amylophagia: consumption of starch

Xerophagy: consumption of dry food

Coprophagia: consumption of feces

Clay

Got a tummy ache? Need to settle the stomach? Kaolin, a mineral dust found in clay, has been used around the world as a digestive aid, especially in Africa and even parts of the rural United States where it is known as "eating chalk" or "white dirt." It is thought that the chalk coats the intestines, absorbing toxins and preventing diarrhea, although this is debatable. Creamy smooth kaolin can still be found in some stores, and it used to be a main ingredient in a popular anti-diarrhea product.

Gold Flakes

All that glitters is not gold, but the shiny stuff sprinkled on cakes and other goodies sure looks like it. Buy edible gold as flakes, sprinkles or even leaf sheets, and rest assured that it is harmless (good to know if you have a gold tooth filling), albeit rather tasteless. Nevertheless, this food decoration jazzes up even the plainest dessert. Twenty-four-karat gold flakes can also be found in specialty chocolates, marmalade, wine, liquors and ice cream. One Scottish restaurateur even created a $4000 pizza with edible gold as a topping. White powdered gold, on the other hand, is an ancient and now New Age substance of legendary status believed to cure a variety of aliments. Also called the "Elixir of Life," "Gold of the Gods" or the "Philosopher's Stone," it's available all over the Internet, but not yet at your local pharmacy, or jewelry, store.

Edible Luxuries

1. A glass of champagne laced with finely crushed pearls and considered an aphrodisiac

2. An edible mini-scorpion encased in a vodka-flavored lollipop

3. A jelly dessert infused with 24-karat gold dust

FRANKEN-FOODS

Artificial Food

Yes, humanity has reached the point where we can now produce fake food. Look no further than your neighborhood supermarket for proof. A quick read of many processed-food ingredient lists is enough to challenge a spelling-bee champion. Certain cheeses never need refrigeration until opened, and even then, they'll stay orange and spreadable for eons. Non-dairy creamers and edible oil products line the dairy section shelves, but most don't contain the tiniest molecule of milk. These foods aren't found only in western cultures, either. Besides the U.S., China and India are among the world's biggest edible oil consumers.

Plastic foods aren't only table decorations; they're entering our food supply. One synthetic product, Olestra, was designed to improve what we already ate. A fake fat with no calories, it was approved for use in 1996 and made a splash in the food world. Junk-food addicts could now eat Olestra-laced potato chips and not worry about fats. Unfortunately, they had a new worry—urgent trips to the bathroom. Olestra's unpleasant side effects caused vitamin loss, and the product never did revolutionize the snack-food world as hoped.

Sugar substitutes are another modern marvel. Several hundred times sweeter than sugar, saccharin was invented over a century ago. Another artificial sweetener, aspartame, can be found in 5000 different foods from diet soda to desserts (incidentally, a by-product of aspartame's manufacture is sold as fertilizer). Both sweeteners tend to leave an aftertaste, but that's not the worst of their problems. As with other synthetic additives, there are fears that these compounds may be linked to allergies and diseases such as cancer.

Carcinogenic worries have also been linked to food irradiation. Since 1963, blasts of radiation have been used to help preserve meats and prevent the fruits and vegetables from sprouting.

Unless we buy from organic suppliers, most of us are resigned to the chemicals added to foods for color, preservation and taste. For instance, a loaf of plain, sliced, white bread contains the following:

> *Unbleached enriched wheat flour, water, glucose-fructose/sugar, *yeast, canola or soya oil, salt, soy flour, sodium stearoyl-2-lactylate, calcium propionate, plant mono and/or diglycerides, calcium carbonate, ammonium chloride, calcium sulfate. May contain acetylated tartaric acid esters of mono and diglycerides, calcium iodate. * Order may change. May contain traces of sesame seeds, milk ingredients and sulfites.*

Trust me, you don't want to even look at the ingredients of an artificially flavored blue raspberry instant drink packet. The definition of "food" is definitely changing. Eat, drink and be wary.

Margarine Nation

In the 1860s, Emperor Napoleon III offered a prize to anyone who could invent a butter substitute. In reality, the military was behind his motive since butter didn't keep well in soldiers' rations (and who wants French bread without fresh, creamy butter). The winner, a chemist named Hippolyte Mège-Mouriés, later became known as the creator of margarine. What Mège-Mouriés invented was oleomargarine or butterine, essentially an edible oil. Today, margarine is made from various oils, including olive, soybean or safflower, and the average American eats twice as much of it as butter. Not surprisingly, the dairy industry fought margarine every slippery step of the way. It supported a ban of margarine's butter yellow coloration and touted its product as all-natural. Margarine manufacturers battled back with "healthier" varieties of their products, including those containing liquid vegetable oils and polyunsaturated instead of saturated fats. The clash of the spreads continues to this day.

Did You Know?

Researchers at a British agricultural institute have produced a genetically modified wheat with fewer calories than other varieties. Flour derived from this wheat is also digested more slowly, making people feel fuller and less likely to consume more. This revolutionary food could help in the fight against obesity, allowing everyone to have their cake and eat it, too.

(*Daily Telegraph*, July 2008)

AVANT-GARDE COOKING

Molecular gastronomy is to future cuisine as microwaving was to the 1960s. Cutting-edge chefs now use anti-griddles (cooktops that freeze instead of heat) or liquid nitrogen to make such artistic delicacies as carrot foam or scrambled egg ice cream. (Time, November 2008)

Space Cuisine

Deep in a restricted high-tech storage facility, securely packaged and neatly labeled foodstuffs patiently await their turn. These vittles are destined to go where no food has gone before—outer space. If you thought packing food for a camping trip was a chore, try planning the menus for space missions. Each ration must be nutritious, easy to prepare and safe to consume in zero gravity. Spill some juice, and it'll float by your face; drop a few crumbs, and they could clog up an air vent. NASA actually tests potential space menus on the KC-135 zero-gravity airplane—the "vomit comet"—to make absolutely sure they're suitable in a space environment. The food must also have an extended shelf life suitable for long-term missions thousands of miles from planet Earth while stored in a space smaller than most beer fridges. What's on the cosmic menu? Not just granola bars or dried fruit, and no longer do astronauts have to squeeze their food out of tubes like beef-flavored doggie toothpaste. How about rehydratable corn flakes, thermostabilized chunky chicken stew, shelf-stable tortillas (no crumbs) or thermostabilized and irradiated beef tips with mushrooms? Nothing is overlooked, including the liquefied salt and pepper. Astronauts don't want to spend time rubbing tiny flakes out of their eyes—they might miss a beautiful Earthrise.

Did You Know?

After their famous first walk on the moon, Neil Armstrong and Edwin "Buzz" Aldrin had roast turkey and trimmings (in space food packets, of course).

Instant Tang

Wanna feel like an astronaut? Drink Tang, er, except this powdered drink wasn't a NASA creation. First marketed in 1959, NASA jumped on this orange-flavored rocket fuel and used it on space flights in 1965 to make water taste better. Now owned by the Kraft company, Tang is still widely available in supermarkets. But don't put these drink crystals in your dishwasher—the citric acid could harm the appliance!

(May Contain) Genetically Modified Organisms

It's becoming a perfect world in the produce department. The tomatoes appear flawless, the bananas are still freshly yellow, and the strawberries look twice as big as they used to. If you don't think you've ever eaten genetically modified organisms (GMOs), think again. Sliced bread, certain vegetables, popcorn, soybeans or canola oil—yes, they've likely had their DNA rearranged. Although GMO labeling in the U.S. and Canada is optional (unlike the UK and many European countries), estimates are that at least 60 percent of processed foods have been genetically altered. Essentially, the genes from a plant or animal—anything with a genetic code—are cut and pasted into another organism that may or may not even be the same species. The results are mind-boggling: tomatoes that are impervious to cold weather, faster-growing fish and crops resistant to insects and stacked with vitamins. Does made-to-order food get any better than this? Environmental groups, however, are concerned because we don't know the long-term consequences of manipulating nature. While the possibilities for GMOs seem endless, it's sobering to realize that DNA digs aren't in the realm of science future—they're already here. By the way, time for lunch. How would you like your transgenic salmon today?

FIT for the GODS

They make headlines and draw pilgrims from around the world. Accounts of divine food intervention seem to be on the rise, but are they quirks of nature or true signs from God? And why doesn't Jesus ever appear on an expensive T-bone steak?

Oh, My Cod!

It started out like any ordinary dinner. A man in Ontario, Canada, grabbed a bag of frozen fish sticks, shook a few onto a baking pan and shoved them into the oven. When he pulled out the pan to flip the sticks over, his jaw dropped. There, in the middle of the burned, brown batter was the contour of a familiar face, and it bore a remarkable resemblance to Jesus.

Holy Cow

The Arabic word for God appeared on cold cuts in a Nigerian restaurant. Thousands of tourists made a pilgrimage to view the miraculous meat and were no doubt very hungry once they reached their destination.

Fruity Faith

In Senegal, a fruit vendor was ecstatic when he discovered that the stripes on one of his watermelons made the name of Allah. A Muslim woman from Sweden was twice as fortunate. She sliced open a mango and saw black lines that formed the Arabic word for Allah on one half and Muhammad on the other.

One Virgin Sandwich, To Go

Just before she bit into her grilled breakfast sandwich one morning, a woman in Florida observed a pattern on it that resembled the Virgin Mary. She later sold it to an Internet casino on eBay for $28,000.

Our Daily Bread

A Florida man spotted the image of Jesus holding a cross, with two birds in the background, on his French toast. He told a local news station that he had no plans to sell the toast but hoped the image would "renew the hope and faith" of those who see it.

Bless This Bun

In 1996, a cinnamon bun bearing the image of Mother Teresa turned a Nashville coffee shop into an international pilgrimage stop. Kept under a glass cover, the famous bun hardened but remained viewable for curious visitors and the baking faithful. Unfortunately, nine years later, it was stolen on Christmas Day.

She's Baaack...on a Grape

A West Virginia woman noticed the figure of the Virgin Mary on a grape. She admitted that she did not expect to see "holy people popping up in our foodstuffs," but after posting a picture on her webpage, she was urged to contact the media about her divine fruit. No word yet on whether the grape has transformed into raisin Jesus.

FOOD FINALE

It's a safe bet to say that humans will keep on eating. We chow down because we're hungry, bored, stressed out and for a million other reasons. In a nutshell, good grub hits the spot like nothing else. For most of western society today, obtaining food is synonymous with grocery shopping, dashing into a convenience store, dropping two bucks in a vending machine or, if we're lucky, checking out a local market. Slam a frozen dinner into the microwave and out pops a gourmet meal. What we buy to eat is more often than not cleaned, packaged, frozen, processed or ready to eat. That's a far cry from our ancestors, who hunted, fished and grew crops for dinner. Many cultures in other countries still get food that way, though large parts of the world's population consider themselves fortunate to have a daily bowl of rice.

Even if all our nutritional needs could be met by popping a pill, would anyone truly want to trade three meals a day for three tablets? The way food looks, smells and tastes is part of the whole sustenance package. But what if you sampled the most delicious dish in the world only to find out it came from something you found repulsive? And (assuming you don't throw up) does your body really care as long as its nutritional needs are met? Weird food is in the eye of the beholder, or more correctly, the diner's mouth. If we go beyond our initial apprehension, we may be pleasantly surprised, and not a minute too soon. The future of food could turn out to be more like the old days before supermarket cities and fast-food restaurants. With the cost of mass-produced cattle, meats may have to move over. It will be time to eat more local plants, veggies, perhaps even grow our own, and seriously consider a fried bug or two. We'll likely be healthier and happier with our brand-new diet. So the next time you come across a new or unusual food, open your mind and your mouth. Enjoy the thrill, and every bite, too!

> Part of the secret of success in life is to eat what you like and let the food fight it out inside.
>
> – Mark Twain

What is the Weirdest Food You Have Ever Eaten?

> "Vietnamese soup with pig stomach, and other stuff I could not identify! That being said, it's amazingly good with Asian chili sauce and cold Vietnamese coffee with sweetened cream."
>
> – David

> "In Namibia...I had a monkey gland burger, not bad, but I found out later it was a springbok (type of deer). The meat was cooked in a sauce that made it kind of like a Sloppy Joe burger. Quite tasty."
>
> – Wayne

> "They fed me a lot of bad food in the army..."
>
> – Mike

"...well, let's see—I had liver pudding (*braunschweiger*) once, long ago. I had Polish duck blood soup...I've had haggis, which was a lot like Thanksgiving oyster dressing made from oatmeal. You just have to forget what the "oysters" really are. My Italian grandma used to make chicken soup with the bright yellow chicken feet! You could walk them across the table. I've tried a lot of forage foods, like cattail root, paw-paws, nasturtium leaves, wild onions, wild asparagus. But that's about it."

– Nick from Ohio

"I find some tofu to be icky, kinda gelatinous and slimy and tasteless. My parents ate turtle leg soup in China and found it to be very odd. Frankly, if something is well cooked, you can eat some potentially very gross and strange stuff and have it taste good."

– Mark

ABOUT THE ILLUSTRATORS

Peter Tyler

Peter Tyler is a graduate of the Vancouver Film School's Visual Art & Design, and Classical Animation programs. Though his ultimate passion is in filmmaking, he is also intent on developing his draftsmanship and storytelling, with the aim of using those skills in future filmic misadventures.

Roger Garcia

Roger Garcia is a self-taught artist with some formal training who specializes in cartooning and illustration. He is an immigrant from El Salvador, and during the last few years, his work has been primarily cartoons and editorial illustrations in pen and ink. Recently he has started painting once more. Focusing on simplifying the human form, he uses a bright minimal palette and as few elements as possible. His work can be seen in newspapers, magazines, promo material and at www.rogergarcia.ca.

ABOUT THE AUTHOR

Joanna Emery

Joanna Emery is the author of many books including *Gross and Disgusting Things About the Human Body* (Blue Bike Books). While writing *Weird Food*, Joanna admits that her tummy growled constantly. She vows to one day travel the world and sample as many of the delicacies she has researched (except the endangered species and fugu, for instance) as she can possibly stomach. Joanna lives with her vegetarian husband and their three pepperoni-pizza-loving children.

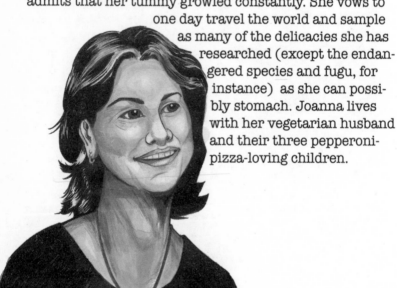